W9-BVL-727

Zebulon Pike
and the Explorers of the American Southwest

General Editor

William H. Goetzmann
Jack S. Blanton, Sr., Chair in History
 University of Texas at Austin

Consulting Editor

Tom D. Crouch
Chairman, Department of Aeronautics
 National Air and Space Museum
 Smithsonian Institution

WORLD EXPLORERS

Zebulon Pike
and the Explorers of the American Southwest

Jared Stallones

Introductory Essay by Michael Collins

CHELSEA HOUSE PUBLISHERS

New York · Philadelphia

On the cover Pike's map of the territory of New Spain; portrait of Zebulon Pike

Chelsea House Publishers
Editor-in-Chief Remmel Nunn
Managing Editor Karyn Gullen Browne
Copy Chief Mark Rifkin
Picture Editor Adrian G. Allen
Art Director Maria Epes
Assistant Art Director Noreen Romano
Series Design Loraine Machlin
Manufacturing Manager Gerald Levine
Systems Manager Lindsey Ottman
Production Manager Joseph Romano
Production Coordinator Marie Claire Cebrián

World Explorers
Senior Editor Sean Dolan

Staff for ZEBULON PIKE AND THE EXPLORERS OF THE AMERICAN SOUTHWEST
Copy Editor Benson D. Simmonds
Editorial Assistant Martin Mooney
Picture Researcher Lisa Kirchner
Senior Designer Basia Niemczyc

Copyright © 1992 by Chelsea House Publishers, a division of Main Line Book Co. All rights reserved. Printed and bound in the United States of America.

3 5 7 9 8 6 4 2

Library of Congress Cataloging-in-Publication Data

Stallones, Jared.
   Zebulon Pike and the explorers of the American Southwest/Jared Stallones.
       p.   cm.—(World explorers)
   Includes bibliographical references and index.
   Summary: A biography of the army officer and explorer who discovered, among other places in the West and Southwest, the great Rocky Mountain peak in Colorado that bears his name.
   ISBN 0-7910-1317-0
         0-7910-1541-6 (pbk.)
   1. Pike, Zebulon, 1779–1813—Juvenile literature.
   2. Explorers—West (U.S.)—Biography—Juvenile literature.
   3. Southwest, New—Discovery and exploration—Juvenile literature.
   4. Southwest, New—History—To 1848—Juvenile literature.
   [1. Pike, Zebulon, 1779–1813. 2. Explorers. 3. Southwest, New—Discovery and exploration.] I. Series.
   F592.P653S73   1991   91-10072
   978′.02′0922—dc20   CIP
   [B]   AC

CONTENTS

Into the Unknown..................................7
Michael Collins

The Reader's Journey..................................9
William H. Goetzmann

ONE   The Cat's-paw..................................13

TWO   The Rascal's Protégé..................................25

        Map: The Expeditions of Zebulon Pike..................32

THREE   To the Source..................................37

FOUR   With Great Circumspection..................................53

FIVE   Lost in the Mountains..................................67

        Picture Essay: Under Western Skies..................73

SIX   Is This Not the Red River?..................................85

SEVEN   Blazing Trails..................................93

        Further Reading..................................105

        Chronology..................................107

        Index..................................109

WORLD EXPLORERS

THE EARLY EXPLORERS

Herodotus and the Explorers of the Classical Age
Marco Polo and the Medieval Explorers
The Viking Explorers

THE FIRST GREAT AGE OF DISCOVERY

Jacques Cartier, Samuel de Champlain, and the Explorers of Canada
Christopher Columbus and the First Voyages to the New World
From Coronado to Escalante: The Explorers of the Spanish Southwest
Hernando de Soto and the Explorers of the American South
Sir Francis Drake and the Struggle for an Ocean Empire
Vasco da Gama and the Portuguese Explorers
La Salle and the Explorers of the Mississippi
Ferdinand Magellan and the Discovery of the World Ocean
Pizarro, Orellana, and the Exploration of the Amazon
The Search for the Northwest Passage
Giovanni da Verrazano and the Explorers of the Atlantic Coast

THE SECOND GREAT AGE OF DISCOVERY

Roald Amundsen and the Quest for the South Pole
Daniel Boone and the Opening of the Ohio Country
Captain James Cook and the Explorers of the Pacific
The Explorers of Alaska
John Charles Frémont and the Great Western Reconnaissance
Alexander von Humboldt, Colossus of Exploration
Lewis and Clark and the Route to the Pacific
Alexander Mackenzie and the Explorers of Canada
Robert Peary and the Quest for the North Pole
Zebulon Pike and the Explorers of the American Southwest
John Wesley Powell and the Great Surveys of the American West
Jedediah Smith and the Mountain Men of the American West
Henry Stanley and the European Explorers of Africa
Lt. Charles Wilkes and the Great U.S. Exploring Expedition

THE THIRD GREAT AGE OF DISCOVERY

Apollo to the Moon
The Explorers of the Undersea World
The First Men in Space
The Mission to Mars and Beyond
Probing Deep Space

CHELSEA HOUSE PUBLISHERS

Into the Unknown

Michael Collins

It is difficult to define most eras in history with any precision, but not so the space age. On October 4, 1957, it burst on us with little warning when the Soviet Union launched *Sputnik*, a 184-pound cannonball that circled the globe once every 96 minutes. Less than 4 years later, the Soviets followed this first primitive satellite with the flight of Yuri Gagarin, a 27-year-old fighter pilot who became the first human to orbit the earth. The Soviet Union's success prompted President John F. Kennedy to decide that the United States should "land a man on the moon and return him safely to earth" before the end of the 1960s. We now had not only a space age but a space race.

I was born in 1930, exactly the right time to allow me to participate in Project Apollo, as the U.S. lunar program came to be known. As a young man growing up, I often found myself too young to do the things I wanted—or suddenly too old, as if someone had turned a switch at midnight. But for Apollo, 1930 was the perfect year to be born, and I was very lucky. In 1966 I enjoyed circling the earth for three days, and in 1969 I flew to the moon and laughed at the sight of the tiny earth, which I could cover with my thumbnail.

How the early explorers would have loved the view from space! With one glance Christopher Columbus could have plotted his course and reassured his crew that the world was indeed round. In 90 minutes Magellan could have looked down at every port of call in the *Victoria's* three-year circumnavigation of the globe. Given a chance to map their route from orbit, Lewis and Clark could have told President Jefferson that there was no easy Northwest Passage but that a continent of exquisite diversity awaited their scrutiny.

In a physical sense, we have already gone to most places that we can. That is not to say that there are not new adventures awaiting us deep in the sea or on the red plains of Mars, but more important than reaching new places will be understanding those we have already visited. There are vital gaps in our understanding of how our planet works as an ecosystem and how our planet fits into the infinite order of the universe. The next great age may well be the age of assimilation, in which we use microscope and telescope to evaluate what we have discovered and put that knowledge to use. The adventure of being first to reach may be replaced by the satisfaction of being first to grasp. Surely that is a form of exploration as vital to our well-being, and perhaps even survival, as the distinction of being the first to explore a specific geographical area.

The explorers whose stories are told in the books of this series did not just sail perilous seas, scale rugged mountains, traverse blistering deserts, dive to the depths of the ocean, or land on the moon. Their voyages and expeditions were journeys of mind as much as of time and distance, through which they—and all of mankind—were able to reach a greater understanding of our universe. That challenge remains, for all of us. The imperative is to see, to understand, to develop knowledge that others can use, to help nurture this planet that sustains us all. Perhaps being born in 1975 will be as lucky for a new generation of explorer as being born in 1930 was for Neil Armstrong, Buzz Aldrin, and Mike Collins.

The Reader's Journey

William H. Goetzmann

This volume is one of a series that takes us with the great explorers of the ages on bold journeys over the oceans and the continents and into outer space. As we travel along with these imaginative and courageous journeyers, we share their adventures and their knowledge. We also get a glimpse of that mysterious and inextinguishable fire that burned in the breast of men such as Magellan and Columbus—the fire that has propelled all those throughout the ages who have been driven to leave behind family and friends for a voyage into the unknown.

No one has ever satisfactorily explained the urge to explore, the drive to go to the "back of beyond." It is certain that it has been present in man almost since he began walking erect and first ventured across the African savannas. Sparks from that same fire fueled the transoceanic explorers of the Ice Age, who led their people across the vast plain that formed a land bridge between Asia and North America, and the astronauts and scientists who determined that man must reach the moon.

Besides an element of adventure, all exploration involves an element of mystery. We must not confuse exploration with discovery. Exploration is a purposeful human activity—a search for something. Discovery may be the end result of that search; it may also be an accident, as when Columbus found a whole new world while searching for the Indies. Often, the explorer may not even realize the full significance of what he has discovered, as was the case with Columbus. Exploration, on the other hand, is the product of a cultural or individual curiosity; it is a unique process that has enabled mankind to know and understand the world's oceans, continents, and polar regions. It is at the heart of scientific thinking. One of its most significant aspects is that it teaches people to ask the right questions; by doing so, it forces us to reevaluate what we think we know and understand. Thus knowledge progresses, and we are driven constantly to a new awareness and appreciation of the universe in all its infinite variety.

The motivation for exploration is not always pure. In his fascination with the new, man often forgets that others have been there before him. For example, the popular notion of the discovery of America overlooks the complex Indian civilizations that had existed there for thousands of years before the arrival of Europeans. Man's desire for conquest, riches, and fame is often linked inextricably with his quest for the unknown, but a story that touches so closely on the human essence must of necessity treat war as well as peace, avarice with generosity, both pride and humility, frailty and greatness. The story of exploration is above all a story of humanity and of man's understanding of his place in the universe.

The WORLD EXPLORERS series has been divided into four sections. The first treats the explorers of the ancient world, the Viking explorers of the 9th through the 11th centuries, and Marco Polo and the medieval explorers. The rest of the series is divided into three great ages of exploration. The first is the era of Columbus and Magellan: the period spanning the 15th and 16th centuries, which saw the discovery and exploration of the New World and the world ocean. The second might be called the age of science and imperialism, the era made possible by the scientific advances of the 17th century, which witnessed the discovery of the world's last two undiscovered continents, Australia and Antarctica, the mapping of all the continents and oceans, and the establishment of colonies all over the world. The third great age refers to the most ambitious quests of the 20th century—the probing of space and of the ocean's depths.

As we reach out into the darkness of outer space and other galaxies, we come to better understand how our ancestors confronted *oecumene*, or the vast earthly unknown. We learn once again the meaning of an unknown 18th-century sea captain's advice to navigators:

> And if by chance you make a landfall on the shores of another sea in a far country inhabited by savages and barbarians, remember you this: the greatest danger and the surest hope lies not with fires and arrows but in the quicksilver hearts of men.

At its core, exploration is a series of moral dramas. But it is these dramas, involving new lands, new people, and exotic ecosystems of staggering beauty, that make the explorers' stories not only moral tales but also some of the greatest adventure stories ever recorded. They represent the process of learning in its most expansive and vivid forms. We see that real life, past and present, transcends even the adventures of the starship *Enterprise*.

The Cat's-paw

The company split up in the early morning on October 28, 1806, not long after daybreak, following a hastily prepared breakfast probably consisting of not much more than coffee and maybe some buffalo meat. The tents had been struck and the few remaining supplies belonging to the expedition, which had been poorly equipped even at its outset, strapped onto the backs of the horses or loaded into two untrustworthy-looking canoes. One of the boats was a large dugout, hewn from the trunk of a single tree, but suitable timber was hard to come by in this part of the Great Plains and the men were forced to make the second vessel by stretching four buffalo skins and two elk hides over a rickety wooden frame. Their shipbuilding skills did not inspire confidence in the U.S. Army officer, Lieutenant James Biddle Wilkinson, who had been deputed, along with five enlisted men, to sail these two canoes from his current location—a campsite on the south side of the Arkansas River, near its great bend in what is today south-central Kansas—downriver to the mighty Mississippi, a journey of almost 700 miles through territory that at this date in American history remained largely unexplored by Americans and Europeans, although it was, as Wilkinson was all too aware, well traveled by several Indian nations. Along the way Wilkinson was to explore and map as much of the countryside as feasible, paying particular attention

In late 1806, Zebulon Montgomery Pike, an officer in the U.S. Army, led an expedition by river and over land from St. Louis across the Rocky Mountains into Spanish territory—the first important official U.S. exploratory foray into the Southwest.

to soil conditions, topology, climate, waterways, and native inhabitants, all for the purpose of evaluating the region's economic, strategic, and settlement potential. Meanwhile, the remainder of the expedition of which Wilkinson was a part, consisting of 14 soldiers—"a damn'd set of rascals," according to their commanding officer—and 2 civilians, was to set out that same day on horseback in the opposite direction—westward, ostensibly in search of the headwaters of the Red River.

Wilkinson harbored little optimism concerning the portion of the mission with which he had been entrusted. He was a courageous and competent officer, but his 20-some years had been plagued by ill health, and he was of a nervous temperament. Still, there was good cause for his current unease, which he delineated in three letters that he penned on the two days immediately preceding his departure down the Arkansas.

The three missives were addressed to Lieutenant Zebulon Montgomery Pike, the expedition's commander; to General James Wilkinson, Pike's superior officer, governor of the recently acquired Louisiana Territory, ranking general in the U.S. Army, mastermind behind the expedition, and the correspondent's father; and to Ann Biddle Wilkinson, his mother. The younger Wilkinson gave all three to Pike shortly before setting out, at ten o'clock, downriver, trusting that Pike would see to their delivery and apparently assuming that his fellow officer or one of his party was likely to return to civilization before he would. Or perhaps, as pessimistic as Wilkinson was about his mission, he simply believed that Pike's chances of survival were greater than his own.

Wilkinson's letter to his mother, headed "Arkansaw River, 27th Oct.06" and addressed to "My Dear Parent," is of a type written by countless young soldiers away from home. In it, Wilkinson briefly acknowledges the danger of his situation—"In a few moments I enter my skin canoe to descend the river, and part with Mr. Pike—the prospect is not as favorable as I wish"—but takes pains to assure his worried mother that he will come through his trials intact. "I look forward to a pleasant voyage," he writes, rather disingenuously, "tho it may be a tedious one, however I shall have the Satisfaction of handing you a correct survey of the Arkansaw and its waters. My health is perfectly good, and my greatest care shall be to preserve it. I may now and then be a little wet, but I have a large store of thick winter cloathing, and a warm Tent. My coffee and tea is still on hand, as are all my herbs & medicines, none of which I have as yet used." In closing, he cautions her that she may not hear from him for some time, but that such silence will not necessarily speak of disaster but springs rather from the exigencies of his mission, which he is honor bound to fulfill: "You must not look for me

Pike and his men usually broke camp to begin the day's march shortly after dawn. They relied on the abundance of wildlife on the plains to keep them in food. Buffalo meat was their most important staple; the animal's tongue and bones were esteemed as particular delicacies. The explorers also used the buffalo's skin to make blankets, robes, shirts, leggings, and moccasins.

This woodcut of the Arkansas River at it appears near the present-day town of Rocky Ford, Colorado, illustrated the memoirs of John Frémont, one of the greatest explorers of the West, who almost 40 years after Pike had done so was also assigned to make a comprehensive survey of the Arkansas and Red rivers. If one includes its innumerable bends, the Arkansas flows for more than 2,000 miles from its source in the Rockies to the mighty Mississippi.

Till Spring—as I am determined to acquire information of the country adjacent to the river." Finally, he asks that his mother believe him to be "Your dutiful & affect. Son" and signs himself, simply, "James."

In his letter to Pike, dated October 26, Wilkinson is more outspoken about the source of his discontent. He begins deferentially, writing that "your instructions relating to my descent of the Arkansaw, have been perused with attention, and as far as is in my power & the means given me, shall strictly be complied with," but then quickly states that he has "a few questions" to ask his commander. "If you should think this a freedom, inconsistent with the principles of subordination, or unprecedented," he assures Pike, "you will please to excuse the error & attribute it to ignorance, not a want of respect for your Opinion, but to a want of confidence in my own."

That said, Wilkinson gets to the heart of the matter. The mission he has been assigned is poorly conceived, and he has been given insufficient means to conduct it successfully. He is undermanned and undersupplied, and he cannot help but wonder why Pike should be taking with him 15 men to conduct his survey of the Red River, while he, Wilkinson, is to be given the services of only 5, particularly when it is his opinion "that a traverse of the Arkansaw, and a Geographical Sketch of the adjacent country, is an object of as much importance to our Executive [the reference is presumably to President Thomas Jefferson, although it could allude to the senior Wilkinson, whose written orders to Pike did not distinguish, in terms of importance, between exploring the Arkansas and surveying the Red], as one of Red river." His lack of numbers makes it unlikely that he could repel even the smallest Indian raiding party, let alone command the sort of respect necessary to bring the tribes to a diplomatic council. The demands of his mission require that he take his time on the river—"to comply with the wish, intention, spirit and letter of the Generals order & your own, I cannot hurry down the river, without making the required observations"—yet he has been given so little ammunition that he has no choice but to speed his journey to a conclusion. The boats are unreliable, yet he has not even been issued tools that would enable him to construct others "if any accident should happen to my shackling and patched canoes." The lateness of the season makes it likely that he and his men will have to winter on the river, but they have been given just one tent, and the lack of proper equipment and Pike's refusal to post to Wilkinson's party one Freegift Stoute, the carpenter whom he had requested, will surely hinder their ability to construct adequate shelter. These oversights, Wilkinson tells his commander, will haunt him, and they should be rectified, if only for Pike's peace of mind: "You will excuse me Sir, when I observe, that your reflections, when at the source of red river, would be more pleasant, when you *considered*, that by the gift of a *Broad ax, adz & drawing Knife* (of which you have *two & more setts*) you prevented a Friend and Brother Soldiers wintering without stores or any thing comfortable."

Wilkinson's letter to his father, apparently written hastily in the early morning hours before his departure on October 28, is even more plainspoken. The circumspection with which he addressed Pike is here absent, and he spares his father none of the details that he had kept from his mother's presumably more delicate sensibilities. "I am now about undertaking a voyage perhaps more illy equipd than any other Officer, who ever was on Command, in point of Stores, Ammunition, Boats & Men," he writes.

> I have a small skin canoe, of 10 feet in length, with a wooden one of the same length capable to carry one man and his baggage—not more I believe—I have 5 men, whose strength is insufficient to draw up my skin canoe to dry—and which must necessarily spoil. I have no grease to pay the seams of my canoe, and was obliged to use my candles, mixed with ashes, for that purpose. My men have no winter cloathing, and two of them no Blankets. . . . I shall pass, the Republican pawnees, the most rascally nation I know . . . and meet in the course of 6 or 7 weeks the Osages & Arkansaws. . . . The river is now full of ice, so much that I dare not put in my canoes—last night we had a considerable fall of Snow. I asked only 6 men & could not get them. Believe me, that I sacredly write the truth, with a coolness & deliberation I never before have done—and Believe me Your Sincerely Affectionate, tho unhappy Son.

Left necessarily unexplained in this correspondence was a tangled web of relationships, particularly the one between Pike and the elder Wilkinson, that would make the Pike expedition one of the strangest and most controversial in the history of American exploration. Virtually from the time Pike returned in July 1807 at the conclusion of his expedition to the American settlement of Natchitoches, in what would become the state of Louisiana, up to the present day, historians, journalists, politicians, and students of exploration have debated his motivations and the full significance of his expedition. How much Lieutenant

Wilkinson knew of the intrigue in which his father and Pike, wittingly or unwittingly, were embroiled is uncertain; the available evidence seems to suggest that he knew little or nothing at all.

For in addition to being the governor of the Louisiana Territory and the virtual commander in chief of U.S. military forces in the West, James Wilkinson was an unmitigated scoundrel, a handsome, charming, silver-tongued schemer who seemingly had a finger in every pie and whose only loyalty was to his own pocketbook. That at age 49 Wilkinson held such lofty and responsible positions, let alone had not been drummed out of the army or forcibly exiled, was something of a miracle, but he possessed an uncanny ability to survive the wreckage of his schemes, owing at least in part to his willingness to betray his coconspirators at the first hint of disaster and a consummate skill at playing both sides against the middle.

His son, in penning his missive of discontent to his father, was probably aware that it was his father's idea, as contained in the official orders for the expedition that had

Plains Indians hunt buffalo. Pike believed the regions watered by the Arkansas to be a "terrestrial paradise" for the "wandering savages" because of the abundance of game, particularly buffalo, to be found there. "There are buffalo, elk, and deer sufficient on the banks of the Arkansaw alone," he wrote, "if used without waste, to feed all the savages in the United States territory one century." On his trip downriver, the younger James Wilkinson reported seeing buffalo herds whose size "surpassed credibility."

been given Pike, that the younger Wilkinson be given command of the Arkansas River portion of the mission. Had his son's letter ever been delivered, General Wilkinson probably would not have been happy to learn that because of a lack of manpower and supplies—charges that Pike, himself hardly the most reliable of sources, denied—his son felt that his life had been endangered. Although one can never be sure of anything in assessing the general's motivations, by most accounts he did hold a genuine paternal affection, maybe even love, for his boy. In all likelihood, however, General Wilkinson would have been relieved to learn that Pike had done as he had ordered and sent the younger Wilkinson downriver, for the survey of the Arkansas provided a cover for what the general regarded as the expedition's most important work—a spying incursion into the Spanish territory of what is now the American Southwest. This aspect of the mission had the approval of the U.S. government and military only to the extent that

The Great Plains give way to tablelands at the foot of the Rocky Mountains, a view that Pike and his men encountered not long after parting company with Wilkinson's party. No artists traveled with Pike's expedition; this engraving is based on a drawing by Samuel Seymour, a member of Stephen Long's 1820 expedition to the same region. Seymour is believed to be the first artist to draw and paint the Rockies from life.

Wilkinson was a high government and military official; certainly, he had cleared it neither with President Jefferson nor with Secretary of War Henry Dearborn. Had he received his son's letter, Wilkinson might even have approved of Pike's distribution of his manpower, for it was the spying mission that the general regarded as most crucial. Wilkinson may even have felt that in having his son sent downriver, no matter how perilous that mission might prove to be, he was sparing him an even greater danger— a winter in the mountains spent searching for and reconnoitering a route to Santa Fe, the Spanish city and trading center located at the foot of the Sangre de Cristo Mountains in present-day New Mexico.

The Spanish prohibited American traders from operating in their vast southwest realm, which at the time encompassed all or part of present-day Texas, New Mexico, Arizona, Utah, Colorado, Nevada, and California, and they were extremely wary of what they perceived as the U.S. government's territorial designs on the region. Disputes over the proper boundaries between the two nations' territories had several times nearly flared into war, and the Spanish were not likely to look kindly upon an American spying mission. Wilkinson's relief at knowing that his son had set off for American territory would thus have been all the greater if, as has been reliably alleged, the general fully intended to betray Pike's expedition to the Spanish.

For complicating matters, as it did everything with which he was involved, was the nefarious character of General Wilkinson's interest in the mission. It was certainly true that a survey of the Red and Arkansas rivers was of some scientific and strategic interest to the young United States. The rivers flowed through the Louisiana Territory, as the massive expanse of real estate west of the Mississippi River that Jefferson had purchased from France in 1803 was known, and had been at best only incompletely explored. Moreover, the Red River was generally

regarded by both the United States and Spain as consti-
tuting a rough boundary between their claims in the
Southwest. Even the secret, spying aspect of the mission,
it could be argued, was in the national interest, as the
government could certainly benefit from any information
obtained about its powerful potential enemy.

Yet for General Wilkinson, national interest was only
a pretense with which to cloak his own devious machinations. For the general and governor was, and had been
for decades, an agent in the pay of Spain, referred to as
Number 13 in secret Spanish diplomatic correspondence.
His disloyalty stemmed not from any ideological conviction or even from personal disappointment of the kind that
had convinced the notorious traitor Benedict Arnold, for
example, with whom Wilkinson had served in the revolutionary war, to betray his nation, but simply from his
realization that by providing the Spanish with information
he could supplement his income and more easily maintain
the sumptuous life-style of which he was enamored. Wilkinson, in fact, felt no more loyalty or affection toward
Spain than he did toward the United States, and the Pike
expedition actually represented his opening move in his
grandest plot of all. With the connivance of Aaron Burr,
the nation's vice-president, whose reputation and political
career were in tatters because of his assassination, in a
duel, of Alexander Hamilton, the former secretary of the
Treasury and the country's most prominent Federalist pol-
itician, Wilkinson was plotting to instigate a war between
the United States and Spain, at which time he and Burr
would lead an army of American filibusters and discon-
tented residents of New Spain (as the Spanish territories
in the Southwest were collectively known) against the
Spanish for the purpose of carving off a chunk of their
territory, in which the vice-president and the governor
would establish their own empire. Pike's spying would
therefore serve Wilkinson in two ways: to provide information that would be valuable when and if an invasion

took place and, particularly if Pike were caught, to create an international incident that might serve to trigger the war Wilkinson desired.

What Pike knew of Wilkinson's true designs remains the great unsolved mystery of this peculiar chapter in the history of American exploration. Was he a willing partner in Wilkinson's grandiose ambition or simply the schemer's dupe, the cat's-paw, a pawn whose inordinate ambition, vanity, and unscrupulousness, combined with the reverence in which he held Wilkinson, who had been a childhood hero and his patron in the military, made him easy prey for a master manipulator? That Pike should be remembered today as an American hero, celebrated as the discoverer of Pikes Peak (which he neither discovered, named, nor climbed) and as an important explorer (he was at best spectacularly unlucky, at worst almost criminally incompetent), is perhaps a fitting historical irony, arising as it does from a venture in which deception was the byword and very little was as it appeared.

From a cactus-strewn bluff, wayfarers look down upon the New Mexico city of Santa Fe. Finding a practical route to Santa Fe in order to establish a trading foothold there was probably one of General James Wilkinson's motives in dispatching Pike toward the Southwest. Santa Fe had been inhabited by the Spanish for almost 200 years by the time Pike reached it.

The Rascal's Protégé

William H. Goetzmann, one of the foremost historians of the exploration of the West, has pointed out that American explorers brought a unique perspective to the 19th-century struggle between the United States and various European powers for control of that portion of North America west of the Mississippi River. One is accustomed to thinking of the vast region between the Mississippi and the Pacific Ocean and south of the 49th Parallel as having always been part of the United States, or at least destined to become so, but in the decades immediately following the establishment of the United States as an independent nation, there was no more certainty that this would be the case than there was that the American experiment in democracy would survive. France, Great Britain, and Spain all had interests in the western lands, and on more than one occasion the United States and one of these European powers came close to war over their conflicting western claims. "For much of the nineteenth century," Goetzmann has written, "it was the explorer out in the wilderness as much as the diplomats in London and Paris and Washington who took the lead in establishing, through his increased geographical knowledge and his control of the Indians, the practical limits of each nation's frontier on the edges of the vast terrestrial sea that lay between them." Far more than his European counterpart, the American explorer was inclined to look at the West in terms of its

As a young officer, Pike recognized that the command of an exploratory expedition would give him the opportunity for glory that was otherwise lacking in the peacetime army. When Pike joined the military, the United States was at peace with its European rivals on the continent and with the Indians of the Old Northwest, leaving him, as he saw it, little chance to distinguish himself.

Aaron Burr as he appeared in later life, a likeness he described as the best produced of him. One of the craftiest—some would say most unscrupulous—politicians produced by the young republic, Burr, then vice-president, saw his political career destroyed following his indictment for murder in New York and New Jersey for the shooting of Alexander Hamilton. He responded to his ruin by hatching a plan to conquer New Spain at the head of an army of frontiersman freebooters.

potential for future settlement as well as for its immediate economic exploitation. This was in large part a product of the American national experience, which had seen settlement move inexorably westward into the unexplored interior, which was inhabited only by the Indians, from its beginnings on the Atlantic seaboard. Americans, to a certain extent, therefore had a frontier perspective; they were used to looking at the wilderness and judging it in terms of land to be settled and all the myriad uses that settlement implies. The European powers were more interested in utilizing the wilderness as a means by which to turn a profit; settlement played a much smaller part in their calculations.

Many of the 19th-century American explorers of the West had experienced frontier living long before they crossed the Mississippi. Zebulon Montgomery Pike was born in present-day Somerset County, New Jersey, on January 5, 1779. He was named after his father, a farmer turned soldier in the Continental army, which was then fighting for the right of the United States, as Britain's 13 former colonies called themselves, to declare its independence; and after General Richard Montgomery, who four years earlier had been killed while leading the failed American campaign against Quebec. Serving under Montgomery on that offensive were three future traitors to the American cause—Benedict Arnold, Aaron Burr, and James Wilkinson. By the time Zebulon Montgomery Pike was born, Wilkinson had already begun his career of infamy by involving himself in the so-called Conway Cabal, a plot to discredit George Washington and force him to resign his position as commander in chief of the Continental army in favor of Horatio Gates, who had been lauded as the hero of the crucial American victory at Saratoga. (In fact, the true hero of Saratoga was Benedict Arnold, and his disgruntlement at being overshadowed by Gates played no small part in his subsequent treason.) Fearful that the cabal was about to be exposed, Wilkinson informed on Gates and General Thomas Conway, his coconspirators, exhibiting for the first time a pattern of behavior that would persist throughout his lifetime.

Zebulon Montgomery was the first child born to Zebulon and Isabella Brown Pike, who had been married four years earlier. He was followed by three others—James Brown Pike, who was disabled by tuberculosis for much of his long life; Maria Herriot Pike, the only girl, who would be in later years her oldest brother's favorite relative; and George Washington Pike, who would die at age 19 in 1793 of the same disease that troubled James. After the revolutionary war, Zebulon Pike moved his growing family to western Pennsylvania, which then constituted the western American frontier, to try his hand at farming once again. Frontier children generally received irregular schooling, and young Zebulon Montgomery was no exception. Although he attended several country grade schools, whatever skill he later exhibited in math, the sciences, and languages (he spoke French in addition to his native tongue) as an army officer attests more to his own native intelligence and drive than to a formal education. Living on the frontier did enable Pike to develop a number of other skills that he would later find indispensable, however: He became a crack shot and a seasoned outdoorsman.

By 1790 the older Zebulon Pike had grown tired of scratching a living from the rocky Pennsylvania soil and had again forsaken agriculture for the military. He obtained a commission as a captain in the Pennsylvania militia, whose most important responsibility was protecting settlers on the frontier against Indian attack. On November 4, 1791, Pike was with a large force, consisting of soldiers from the Pennsylvania, Kentucky, and Virginia militias, that was overwhelmed by an Indian attack near present-day Greenville, Ohio. The poorly trained American soldiers broke and ran before the Indian onslaught; the resulting massacre so frightened western settlers that

Congress was forced to dispatch the regular army for the defense of the frontier. Pike left the militia for a post under General "Mad" Anthony Wayne, the head of the U.S. military in the West. In April 1793, he moved his entire family with him to his new post at Fort Washington, near present-day Cincinnati, Ohio. Making his headquarters at the fort was the second-ranking general in the army, James Wilkinson.

In his two-tone dress uniform covered with gold braid, the handsome Wilkinson was a heroic figure to the younger Zebulon Pike, then an impressionable youth of 14, but his charm masked a sinister character and nefarious designs. After the Conway Cabal had been brought to light, Wilkinson had been made to resign his commission, but the Continental army's need for experienced officers soon overrode his superiors' qualms about his character and he quickly received a new assignment, with a promotion to general. Two years later, in 1781, he again resigned from the service and lit out for the frontier along the Ohio River in Kentucky, where the opportunities for an energetic, intelligent, ambitious, and unscrupulous individual were limitless. Wilkinson achieved considerable economic success as a farmer and merchant—his spread was located on the opposite side of the Ohio from Fort Washington—and attained political prominence as a leader in the movement to make Kentucky a state.

Farmers and merchants on the Ohio River frontier were most concerned that the Mississippi River, into which the Ohio flowed, be open to U.S. navigation for its entire length. It would be in many ways easier, not to mention more profitable, for the settlers on the frontier if they could float their goods down the Ohio and the Mississippi to market in the Spanish city of New Orleans rather than carry them to market over the difficult overland routes to the American cities on the Atlantic seaboard. Their goods were also likely to fetch a higher price in New Orleans than elsewhere. Spain, which traditionally kept a stranglehold over its possessions in North America, resisted this idea and prohibited American traders from bringing their goods to New Orleans, and the eastern political and economic interests in the United States were not overly concerned with securing freedom of navigation down the Mississippi, which they correctly foresaw would cut into their own commerce.

The rascally Wilkinson saw opportunity for profit in this situation. In 1787 he went to New Orleans, where he met with the Spanish governor, Esteban Miro, and promised his help in fomenting a rebellion in Kentucky that would detach that territory and other western regions from the grasp of the United States and place them in the arms of Spain. In exchange, Miro gave Wilkinson the right to ship $30,000 worth of goods through New Orleans each year. While there, Wilkinson swore an oath of allegiance to the Spanish crown. His scheme, however, went for naught. Kentucky's settlers, many of whom had fought for the American cause during the revolutionary war, were not especially interested in becoming colonial subjects of the Spanish monarchy, and Spain's king, when he received Miro's report of the affair, proved not especially interested in precipitating a contretemps with the United States. Still,

Fort Washington was erected in 1789 on the Ohio River at the site of what is today the city of Cincinnati, Ohio. Pike's father moved his entire family to the fort and nearby settlement when he was posted there in 1793.

Wilkinson was able to persuade Miro to pay him a sizable annual retainer in exchange for information, often spurious, that he provided the Spanish on U.S. designs on the Southwest. He had become Spain's agent Number 13.

He never stopped scheming. In early 1794, not long after the Pikes had arrived at Fort Washington, Wilkinson resurrected his rebellion plot for the benefit of Baron Francisco Luis Hector de Carondelet, Miro's successor, thereby extracting from him a hefty payment in addition to his yearly stipend. Simultaneously, the roguish general made use of a ne'er-do-well horse smuggler and adventurer named Philip Nolan, who was in the habit of operating within Spanish territory, to gather military and political intelligence on the Spanish. At the same time, Wilkinson was busy spreading calumny about General Wayne, whom he hoped to replace as the army's ranking general. But nature proved more effective than his slanderous tongue in helping him attain that goal: When Wayne died in December 1796, Wilkinson became the commanding general of the U.S. Army.

Among his subordinates was the younger Zebulon Pike, who two years earlier, at the age of 15, had enlisted as a cadet in his father's company. Having grown up hearing tales of military bravery and derring-do, Pike desperately coveted glory. "You will hear of my fame or my death," he would crow vaingloriously almost two decades later at the outbreak of the War of 1812, and the same fever no doubt burned as strongly in him as a youth just embarking on his martial career.

Despite his later (and unverified) claims to have taken part in the Battle of Fallen Timbers, at which Wayne's troopers crushed the power of the Old Northwest tribes (the Miami, the Shawnee, the Ottawa, and the Potawatomi), Pike's initial opportunities for fame were few, however. For the next several years, he was assigned the vital but glamourless tasks of a quartermaster, the army officer responsible for supplying a body of troops. Primarily, he

transferred supplies by barge and keelboat between Fort
Washington and his father's new command at Fort Mas-
sac, located on the Ohio some 40 miles east of its junction
with the Mississippi. Although Pike itched for more ex-
citing duty, his assignment did afford him the opportunity
to gain valuable experience at wilderness command.

Once Wilkinson took command of the army, his youth-
ful admirer and protégé advanced more rapidly through
the ranks. On March 3, 1799, Pike was promoted to second lieutenant, and he received his promotion to full lieutenant just eight months later. By this point, his essential
character was already fairly well formed: Pike was extremely ambitious; more gifted intellectually than many
of his compatriots in the western army; discreet; abstemious
regarding food and drink; rigid to the point of sanctimony
concerning the behavior of others, especially drunkenness
and sexual debauchery; a strict disciplinarian not averse to
using corporal punishment to enforce his command. At
least one biographer has described him as prudish; certainly his generally more rollicking fellow soldiers found
his distaste for roistering somewhat unusual. He seems to
have inspired loyalty among those he commanded chiefly
as the result of his willingness to share more or less equally
with his subordinates in any danger or hardship faced
rather than from individual charisma or any extraordinary
force of personality. There are no surviving contemporary
accounts that indicate that Pike was exceptionally persua-
sive or eloquent verbally, and his surviving writing is un-
remarkable. He stood five feet eight inches tall, "tolerably
square and robust," according to another officer, "his com-
plexion was ruddy, eyes blue, light hair and good features
. . . very gentlemanly in his deportment, manner agreeable and polished, rather reserved in general. . . . No
officer could be more attentive, prompt and efficient . . .
nor was there any more emulous to acquire a perfect
knowledge of the military profession, nor more zealous,
ardent and persevering in the pursuit of scientific improve-

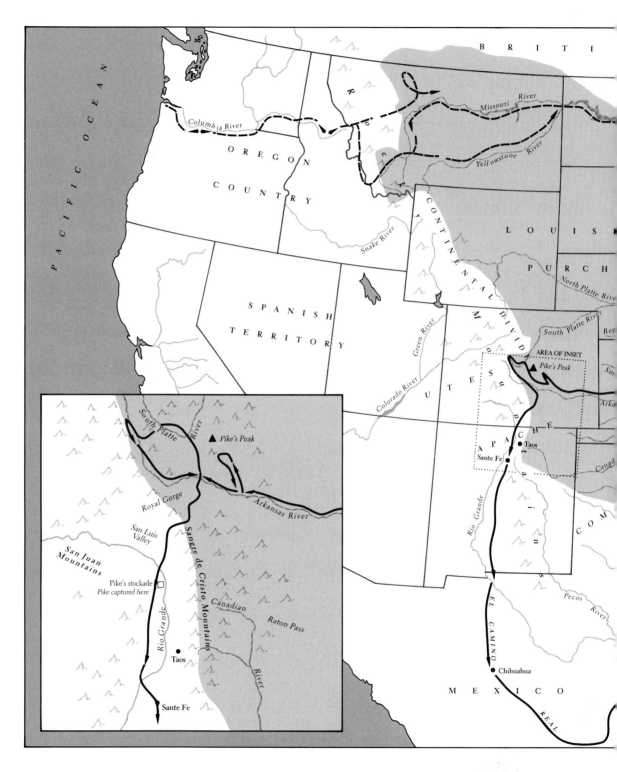

PACIFIC OCEAN

B R I T I

Missouri River

Yellowstone River

O R E G O N

C O U N T R Y

Columbia River

Snake River

L O U I S

P U R C H

North Platte River

South Platte River

Rep

CONTINENTAL DIVIDE

AREA OF INSET

▲ Pike's Peak

S P A N I S H

T E R R I T O R Y

Green River

Colorado River

U T E S

Arka

A P A C H E

● Taos

Sante Fe ●

Rio Grande

C O M

Canad

Pecos River

EL CAMINO

● Chihuahua

M E X I C O

REAL

Inset map:

South Platte River

▲ Pike's Peak

Royal Gorge

Arkansas River

San Luis Valley

San Juan Mountains

Sangre de Cristo Mountains

Pike's stockade ☐
Pike captured here

Rio Grande

Canadian River

Raton Pass

● Taos

→ Sante Fe

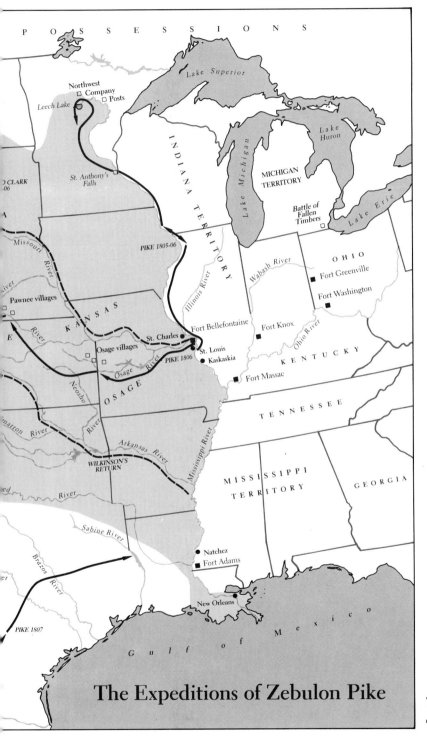

The Expeditions of Zebulon Pike

The route of Pike's two exploratory expeditions.

ment. . . . He had acquired by his own persevering industry a tolerably good knowledge of the French language."

During the years he spent plying the Ohio, Pike got into the habit of stopping at the small river settlement of Sugar Grove, Kentucky, some 15 miles below Cincinnati. The attraction this hamlet held for the serious young lieutenant was Clarissa Brown, Pike's cousin on his mother's side, a tall, shy, austere young woman who lived on a nearby plantation. Pike relished his conversations with the well-educated Clara, as he affectionately called her, and the two fell in love. In 1801, he proposed marriage, but Clarissa's very wealthy father, Captain James Brown, opposed the match, believing his daughter could do better in matrimony than a penniless lieutenant. Undaunted, Pike and his beloved eloped to Cincinnati. Their marriage

President Thomas Jefferson was interested in western exploration both as a means of advancing scientific knowledge and as a necessary diplomatic and strategic initiative aimed at securing the western lands for the United States.

caused a rift between the Pikes and the Browns, but Clarissa remained a constant source of strength and encouragement to her husband, despite a great deal of tremendous personal sorrow. Of the five children born to the Pikes, only one would survive to adulthood.

For several years after their marriage, Pike and his bride moved often, as, at the behest of Wilkinson, the lieutenant was posted to several different stations. Pike served at Fort Knox, on the Wabash River near Vincennes, Indiana; at Wilkinsonville in Illinois; and at Kaskaskia, 150 miles west of Fort Knox, near the junction of the Kaskaskia River and the mighty Mississippi, where he commanded for a while. Wilkinson also used him several times to carry dispatches to Washington, D.C., but the routine-filled and notoriously rowdy life of an army garrison did not suit Pike well, and he longed for a more glamorous assignment. Enormous changes were occurring on the frontier. American settlement was pushing inexorably westward, to the Mississippi and even beyond; then in his late sixties, the legendary and indefatigable American explorer Daniel Boone, who had literally blazed the most important road from the Atlantic Coast over the Appalachians, had at the turn of the century crossed the Father of Waters and claimed a spread in what would become Missouri, and he continued to roam even farther afield. In 1803, Boone's new home became U.S. territory. That year, to the amazement of the American envoys sent to negotiate with his government, Napoléon Bonaparte of France had agreed to sell the United States the Louisiana Territory, an enormous expanse of land that stretched from the Gulf of Mexico to the 49th Parallel and from the Mississippi River to the Rocky Mountains, thereby abandoning his plans to establish an extensive New World empire. The acquisition all but guaranteed that the United States would continue to expand to the west; it meant as well a new world of opportunity for men such as James Wilkinson and Zebulon Pike.

Musket fire hails the raising of the American flag at New Orleans on March 10, 1804, marking the official transfer of the Louisiana Territory to the United States. Because Spain had transferred Louisiana to France such a short time prior to Napoléon's sale of the territory to the United States, many of Spain's government officials and institutions were still in place there at the time of the transfer, and the Spanish continued to claim rights and interests in the region.

To the Source

President Thomas Jefferson and the Congress were now faced with the task of administering the vast lands the United States had acquired. For administrative purposes, the Louisiana Territory was divided in two. The smaller area south of the 33rd Parallel was called the Orleans Territory; the much larger expanse north of the 33rd Parallel was called the Louisiana Territory or Upper Louisiana. The governors of the new regions were the same two men who had represented the United States as commissioners at the formal ceremonies during which France officially turned over possession of its western lands. William Charles Coles Claiborne, a former congressman from Tennessee and governor of the Mississippi Territory, was appointed governor of the Orleans Territory; Wilkinson, who had assiduously lobbied Vice-President Burr for the position, was made governor of Upper Louisiana.

As the commanding general of the army and the governor of Upper Louisiana, which encompassed all or part of 14 future states, Wilkinson was now the most powerful man in the West, and his new position gave him increased stature with the Spanish. For Wilkinson, power meant profit; already, he had pocketed $12,000 from his Spanish confidants by selling them what he claimed to be secret plans, made privy to him upon his assuming the commissioner's position, for a U.S. invasion of the Spanish Southwest. The plans were fraudulent, but the Spanish gold was real.

An Osage chief. The St. Louis merchant René Auguste Chouteau, the city's most prominent and prosperous citizen, owed his riches to the trade in pelts with the Osage. Chouteau's influence among the Osage was so great that he was able to persuade a large group of them to break away from the main tribe and establish themselves along the Arkansas River, where they traded exclusively with him.

With his stepfather, Pierre Laclède, the 14-year-old René Auguste Chouteau (pictured), usually referred to as Auguste, helped found the city of St. Louis in 1764. The city was initially conceived as an outpost for the western expansion of the fur trade; by the early 1800s it was the usual jumping-off point for western expeditions of both the entrepreneurial and exploratory variety.

The wily Wilkinson found other ways to profit as well. He made his new headquarters in St. Louis, the Mississippi River city that since its founding in 1764 had been the center of the fur trade in the West. There, he found that his interests coincided with those of René Auguste Chouteau, one of the founders of the city and patriarch of a fur-trading clan that had made its fortune in commerce with the Osage Indians. Chouteau recognized that the change in government of Louisiana would mean increased competition in the local fur trade, which he had theretofore all but monopolized. Already, all sorts of adventurers were congregating in St. Louis with various schemes to exploit the virgin lands to the west. Chouteau petitioned Jefferson to be granted sole control over the issuance of the licenses that allowed individuals to trade legally with the Indians, which would in effect give him control over the fur trade, but the president refused him. (At the time, the actual trapping of fur-bearing animals and the preparation of their pelts was done by the Indians, who then brought the skins either to St. Louis or established trading posts, where they were paid in trade goods for their furs and labor. The importance of the Indians to a fur-trading industry organized along these lines is one reason why, to a certain extent, the United States and the European powers in the West were concerned with cultivating peaceful relations with them. The trade in furs, which existed to satisfy fashionable Europe's hunger for beaver hats and fur trimmings on other sartorial accessories, was enormously lucrative.)

Wilkinson thought that he might be able to help Chouteau out. As governor of Louisiana, he held the power to issue Indian trading licenses. Although he could not give Chouteau what the president had denied him, he could see to it that no licenses were distributed to traders who intended to operate in areas where the Chouteaus, father and sons, had interests. In exchange, the governor would become a very silent partner in the family business.

Jefferson, meanwhile, was most concerned with obtaining an accurate assessment of the character and potential of his country's newly acquired territory, about which very little reliable geographic information existed. His most immediate concern was with the northern reaches of the purchase, specifically those regions traversed and watered by the Missouri River and its tributaries. It was believed that the Missouri stretched almost as far as a range of "Stoney," or Rocky, mountains in the west. What Jefferson wanted to know was whether it was possible, via the Missouri and nearby waters, to cross these mountains and reach the Pacific Ocean. The reader should realize that there were no reliable maps of the continent west of the Mississippi and that very few white men had traveled there extensively; neither Jefferson, who was in all likelihood the most well read man in the country, nor anyone else, for that matter, had even a reliable estimate of the distance between St. Louis and the Rockies, for example, let alone the nature of the terrain intervening.

To obtain the information the government needed, in 1804 Jefferson dispatched two career army officers, Meriwether Lewis and William Clark, at the head of a party of 40-some men—the Corps of Discovery—to make a survey of the land in question. Their orders were comprehensive; the object of their mission, as the president explained in his famous letter to Lewis, was "to explore the Missouri river, & such principal stream of it, as, by it's course & communication with the waters of the Pacific Ocean, may offer the most direct & practicable water communication across this continent, for the purposes of commerce." They were to make a variety of scientific measurements and readings, all of which were to be scrupulously recorded; they were to meet with and observe the native peoples inhabiting the country they passed through, taking pains to lay the groundwork for harmonious relations between the Indian nations and the United States; they were to carefully observe and record their impressions of the climate, terrain, soil, flora, and fauna of the West, with an eye toward both economic exploitation and future settlement.

Exploration was also on the mind of James Wilkinson, who at about the same time that he was informing the Spanish that they ought to halt and detain an American spying mission headed by Lewis and Clark that was about to pass through their lands—the governor was again peddling disinformation, as Lewis and Clark traveled far north of Spanish-claimed territory—was preparing to send out his own expeditions. Much experience at treachery had enabled Wilkinson to refine his peculiar genius, so that his underhanded machinations—or at least his visible actions—were to be henceforth always cloaked in the guise of national interest. The governor saw no reason why his own and the nation's interests could not coincide. Jefferson and the Congress wanted the western lands explored; Wilkinson (or his dupes) would explore them. The information his explorers obtained—on geography, on the Indian tribes, on the best locations for forts—would benefit the nation, but they would also help the governor in his various other ventures.

In August 1805, therefore, Wilkinson dispatched two exploring expeditions from St. Louis. One, led by Lieutenant George Peter, was to travel westward along the Osage River to the villages of the Osage Indians, which were located near the present-day border of Missouri and Kansas. The purpose of Peter's mission, Wilkinson explained in his letter to Secretary of War Henry Dearborn— a missive he was careful to post so that it would reach Washington, D.C., long after Peter had departed, too late for the governor's superiors to countermand his orders, had they wanted to—was "to ascertain the most commanding Sites for Military Posts . . . to ascertain the nature and extent of the Navigation, modes of Commerce, properties of the Soil, quality of water & Species of Timber, with whatever else may be deemed worthy of note."

At Jefferson's direction, Meriwether Lewis (left) and William Clark (right) led an expedition of exploration from St. Louis up the Missouri to its headwaters, then across the Rocky Mountains and down the Columbia River to the Pacific Ocean. Their journals and maps provided the most comprehensive view yet of the peoples, climate, topography, geography, flora, and fauna of the West.

Left unsaid was that the information gathered by Peter would also greatly benefit Wilkinson and his new partners in the fur trade. Peter was also to attempt to win the friendship of the Comanche, because, according to Wilkinson, "they constitute the most powerfull Nation of Savages on this Continent, and have it in their power to facilitate or impede our march into Mexico, should such movement ever become Necessary." But Wilkinson was not content to wait for his government to move against Spain in the Southwest. He and Burr had already launched their treasonous plot, and as Secretary of War Dearborn was reading Wilkinson's letter, the former vice-president, in disgrace for his assassination of Alexander Hamilton, was floating down the Ohio and the Mississippi to New Orleans, attended by 10 army privates, on a barge assigned to his use by Wilkinson.

A second exploring expedition also left St. Louis in August 1805, one that Dearborn also learned about only after it had departed. This mission was led by Lieutenant Zebulon Pike, who had at last obtained the sort of glamorous assignment he had long craved. Pike's mission, as ordered by Wilkinson, was to travel up the Mississippi and its northern tributaries by keelboat for the purpose of determining the great river's source, which was then unknown. The question was of some scientific, if not critical, importance to the nation, but of equal interest to Wilkinson was a purpose that he did not reveal to Dearborn. Pike was also to gather as much information as he could about the state of the fur trade in the region of the northern Mississippi and, while he was at it, bring the British fur traders operating in the region under control by making them pay U.S. duties, cease flying the British flag, and stop presenting medals embossed with the likeness of His Royal Majesty George III to the Indians as gifts. Whereas it would no doubt be appreciated by Jefferson, Dearborn, and the Congress, the information on the fur trade would certainly be equally, if not more greatly, valued by the

Chouteaus and others with a pecuniary interest in expanding their trading interests northward.

How much Pike knew about Wilkinson's true character and designs remains a subject of considerable historical speculation. By all accounts, he held Wilkinson in extremely high personal and professional regard, viewing him as a mentor and friend—"You see, my dear general, I write you like a person addressing a father: at the same time I hope you will consider me not only in a professional, but a personal view, one who holds you in the highest respect and esteem," he wrote Wilkinson from the upper Mississippi in September 1805—and he was zealous, once the governor's plots were finally exposed, in defending him. Such zealousness, it might be argued, could stem as well from Pike's desire to protect his own reputation, but his efforts went far beyond protesting his own innocence. Thus, Pike was not content to proclaim himself an unwitting officer who had merely followed the orders of his commander, but sought to exculpate Wilkinson completely, which suggests, perhaps, that he was well aware that his patron had something to hide. In an interrogatory taken from him years later, when all of Wilkinson's official doings were being examined for evidence of corruption and graft, Pike attested that the idea and authorization for the Mississippi expedition had come not from Wilkinson but from Meriwether Lewis, whom Pike had earlier met at Kaskaskia. While Lewis was preparing for his departure to the West, Pike testified, "he wrote me a letter, informing me it was the intention of the government of the United States, to detach several of the most enterprising officers on different routes, to explore our newly acquired territory of Louisiana, and inquired if it would be agreeable for him to recommend me for one of those commands, to which I applied in the affirmative." Accordingly, when Wilkinson then ordered him north, Pike "conceived" the assignment "to be a continuance of the designs of the government, as suggested to me by governor Lewis."

(Lewis eventually succeeded Wilkinson as governor of the Louisiana Territory.) This somewhat unlikely although not altogether implausible account could neither be confirmed nor denied, for Pike could not produce Lewis's letter to him, and by the time of the interrogatory Lewis was dead, a suicide.

Most likely, Pike recognized that his commanding officer was not squarely on the up-and-up, if not the full extent of his rascality—that is, that the general was a charlatan, but not a traitor—but Wilkinson's skill at blending his own designs with legitimate national pursuits allowed him as well as the general an out. Pike had for many years been desperate for a command that would bring him fame, and he realized that exploring expeditions were a likely road to glory. (He was intensely jealous of Lewis, for example, whose initial dispatches from the upper Missouri had already earned him kudos by the time Pike departed, and it is revealing that in his interrogatory he states that only the "most enterprising officers" were to be offered

Front Street, along the Mississippi in St. Louis. The Chouteau warehouse is about halfway down the thoroughfare.

commands of western expeditions, thereby placing himself in that exclusive category.) Whatever the general was secretly up to did not necessarily have to concern Pike; he could simply follow orders and maintain a reasonably clear conscience, for Wilkinson's interests always coincided, to a certain extent, with the nation's. If the general would profit from Pike's Mississippi expedition, so would the nation gain, and so would Pike's career and quest for fame advance. And even if it could be proved, concerning later events in the explorer's life, that he was aware that Wilkinson was working toward fomenting a war with Spain, could it not be argued that such a war was in the national interest? Certainly, there were many in the nation who felt so. Although the term Manifest Destiny was not used until the 1840s, it was being born as an idea at the same time that the first U.S. exploring expeditions were heading west.

So Pike set about preparing himself for his journey. He moved his family to St. Louis and hurriedly assembled a force of 20 men—17 privates, 2 corporals, and a sergeant. His experience as a supply officer helped him procure, for $2,000, the flour, cornmeal, pork, salt, and whiskey that would serve as the expedition's staples; much of the meat his men would eat would be obtained by hunting. From that same sum, he also purchased lead, paper, ink, flags, hunting dogs, a tent, clothing, and blankets, as well as knives, cloth, and other trinkets to be used as gifts for the Indians. (The exchange of presents was the traditional opening and closing ritual of any diplomatic encounter with the Indians.) He was much less well equipped for the scientific investigation that was the expedition's ostensible purpose—a watch, a thermometer, and an instrument for determining latitude constituted the expedition's only scientific tools. Indeed, as it turned out, the expedition was underequipped for any purposes. Pike anticipated that the mission would take four months to complete; instead, it lasted closer to nine. Nevertheless, by August 9, 1805—

very late in the year to begin a voyage to the Mississippi's headwaters, which begin to freeze in October, but a good time to depart if one wished to encounter fur traders at work, as the autumn was the prime fur-gathering season— all these provisions and supplies were loaded onto the 70-foot keelboat that would carry the expedition upriver from Fort Bellefontaine, a stockade just a short distance above St. Louis.

Taking a keelboat up the Mississippi was very hard work, as the long, low, covered vessel had to be rowed, towed from shore by a rope, or poled along against the current. The men rose on a typical day at about six in the morning and traveled for several hours before stopping for breakfast. Several hours' more work ensued before a halt was called for the large midday meal, usually at about one o'clock. By late afternoon, Pike or one of his fellow officers would be looking for a suitable campsite for the night along the riverbank; the men usually ate their supper around six. Such a long day and intense physical labor made for ravenous appetites and powerful thirsts: On the early part of the journey, before winter set in and game became scarce, each man received seven pounds of meat a day, most of it freshly killed along the shore. Buffalo, elk, and deer meat was highly prized by the expedition's hunters; in leaner times opossum, rabbit, pheasant, or duck would do. Often, the meat was boiled with flour, wild rice, or cornmeal to make a stew. Although such a diet sounds unhealthy by today's nutritional standards, it enabled the men to maintain the strength they needed. The explorers cut the dust in their throats with whiskey, of which they received an increased ration, for reasons of morale, on days when meat was scarce.

Pike's most significant achievement of the expedition took place on September 23, six weeks after the party had left Fort Bellefontaine. On that day, he held a council with the Sioux Indians who lived in the region and persuaded them to sell his government some 100,000 acres, in exchange for future hunting rights and $200 worth of trade goods. The land would become the future site of present-day Minneapolis–St. Paul; more immediately, it became the location of Fort Snelling, the most important U.S. military institution on the upper Mississippi.

Again, the question of Pike's motives and whatever secret understandings he may have reached with Wilkinson

A herd of buffalo graze on the high plains. This engraving was made from a drawing by Seth Eastman, an army officer and art instructor at West Point who began his work depicting the West while stationed at Fort Snelling, the U.S. military installation established on land purchased by Pike from the Sioux on his expedition to the source of the Mississippi.

become important in assessing the expedition, and again definitive answers are hard to come by. He and his men were able to proceed only about 100 miles up the Mississippi above the site of the council with the Sioux before the river froze. Wilkinson's orders instructed him "to ascend the main branch of the River, until you reach the source of it" or until "the waters are froze up." He carried

A Sioux raiding party prepares to leave camp. The name Sioux is a French corruption of the pejorative appellation given the tribe by its Ojibwa enemies—Nadoweisiw, which means Little Snakes. The Sioux called themselves the Otceti Cacowin, which means Seven Council Fires, a reference to their seven tribal divisions. On his Mississippi expedition, Pike encountered Santee Sioux, members of the tribe's easternmost branch.

enough provisions only for four months, two of which were spent. In adherence with his official orders and for the safety of his men, it would seem, he should have returned home; even Wilkinson, perhaps disingenuously, complained in late November in a letter to Dearborn that Pike was stretching his orders and would now not be back until spring.

Yet Pike pressed on, driven either by his own determination to fulfill Wilkinson's secret agenda regarding the fur trade or by his own vainglorious belief that to discover the source of the Mississippi would be to assure himself the fame he craved. The keelboat had been abandoned in favor of canoes, which in turn gave way to sleds that the men pulled over the frozen waterways. As the expedition slogged northward across the wintry landscape, whiskey became increasingly important as a morale booster, and fresh meat grew increasingly difficult to obtain. Only Pike had a tent to sleep in; at night his men huddled and shivered around the campfire. Most days, the party was able to make only a few miles; "never did I undergo more fatigue," its commander wrote in his journal on one of those rare nights when the ink did not freeze in its bottle. By Christmas, the expedition had reached present-day Brainerd, Minnesota, and Pike rewarded his men by granting them each two extra pounds of meat and flour, an increased whiskey ration, and some tobacco. The ink flowed again one night in early January, but, as Pike recorded, "some of the men had their noses . . . fingers, and . . . toes frozen." They continued northward.

By January 30, 1806, Pike and his gallant men had followed the diminishing and frozen Mississippi deep into present-day north-central Minnesota. When the river forked, Pike followed its western branch, which led him and his band of explorers to Lake Leech, believed by many and duly proclaimed by Pike to be the river's source. Unfortunately, as a member of his party, Henry Rowe Schoolcraft, would prove several decades later, he had chosen

Eastman's painting of Fort Snelling, which was established near the Falls of St. Anthony on land purchased by Pike from the Sioux. Much later, this region would become the site of the city of Minneapolis–St. Paul.

incorrectly: The great river's true source, Lake Itasca, lay 25 miles away, at the end of the northwest fork, past Winnibigoshish Lake and Cass Lake.

But Lake Leech, which Pike reached at midafternoon on February 1, did happen to be the winter headquarters of Hugh McGillis, an executive of the North West Company, a British fur-trading concern whose operatives Wilkinson was eager to oust from American territory. From his nearby camp, Pike sent McGillis a long letter, some-

A fur trapper at work. General Wilkinson sent Pike north, at least in part, to discourage the trappers and traders of the North West Company, a fur-trading firm established in Montreal in 1783. According to historian Peter C. Newman, "the North West Company was the first North American business to operate on a continental scale." Its approximately 100 outposts stretched from Montreal to the Pacific and were "connected by an inland navy of 2,000 canoeists."

what extraordinary in its presumptuousness. He "had been dispatched with discretionary orders," Pike wrote, to investigate the North West Company's operations and had discovered, to his dismay, the concern's "commerce and establishments, extending beyond our most exaggerated ideas. . . . I find your establishments at every suitable place. . . . Our traders to the south . . . complain to our government, with justice, that the members of the N. W. company, encircle them on their frontiers . . . and trade with the savages on superior terms." He was authorized to take as strong action, Pike advised, as "strict justice would demand . . . total confiscation of your property, personal imprisonment and fines."

Pike's message, backed as it was by a force of 20 uniformed U.S. soldiers, implied that he was acting at the behest and on the behalf of his government, which, however much it would benefit from the regulation of foreign traders operating in its territory, had in fact little inkling that Pike was issuing threats in its name. But McGillis, who possessed much experience at frontier diplomacy, was uncowed. The North West Company, he informed Pike, would comply with his requests. All duties required by the U.S. government would be paid, the British flag would no longer fly over North West Company outposts on U.S. soil, he would cease holding councils with the Indians for the purpose of winning their allegiance to Britain and his company, and the company would conform to "all rules and regulations of trade that may be established according to common justice." Finally, Pike's bravery in making his journey would "ever be preserved in the annals of the N.W. Company."

No blandishment could have been better calculated to appeal to the glory-seeking lieutenant. Mollified, his mission completed, Pike set out on February 18 for St. Louis, which he reached on April 30 after stopping several times for councils with the Sioux, the Chippewa, and the Menominee, the results of which were insignificant.

With Great Circumspection

If Pike expected that his presumed discovery of the Mississippi's source would win him fame comparable to Lewis's, he was destined to be disappointed. His feat was little more than a footnote to Jefferson's address to Congress on the Lewis and Clark expedition, whose members, after being given up for lost by many, at last returned to St. Louis in September 1806, having become the first Americans to cross the Rockies and reach the Pacific by an overland route. "Very useful additions have also been made to our knowledge of the Mississippi by Lieutenant Pike, who ascended to its source," Jefferson appended to his lengthy report on the achievements of Lewis and Clark. Pike's resentment may be inferred from the numerous subsequent references in his correspondence and journals to Lewis, virtually all of which expressed a certain jealousy.

Yet by the time Jefferson expressed his approval of Lewis and Clark's efforts, Pike was already well engaged in another exploratory enterprise of his own. Just three days after his return to St. Louis, Wilkinson confided in his protégé his intention to send him to the southwest, toward Spanish territory, on a survey of the Arkansas and Red rivers. Pike spent the next several months with Clara, writing his reports of the Mississippi expedition, which he submitted to Wilkinson on July 2, and preparing for his new mission. The latter duty seems to have occupied the greater part of his energies, as his maps and written report

An Osage woman and child. More than one 19th-century American visitor to the Osage described them as being among the most handsome of Indian tribes. Pike reported that Osage women were responsible for almost all the tribe's agriculture, which consisted of growing corn, beans, and pumpkins.

were for the most part indifferently done and imparted very little, if any, significant new information. Much of his geographic material was wrong, and he was not above cribbing data from Clark's monumental report on the Indians living between the Rockies and the Mississippi and presenting it as his own. He seems to have recognized the inadequacy of his efforts; in presenting his "reports, journals, and observations" to Wilkinson, he explained that he had "scarcely returned to St. Louis, before the voyage now in contemplation was proposed to me, and after some consideration, my duty—and inclination in some respects—induced me to undertake it. The preparations for my new voyage prevented the possibility of my paying that attention to the correction of my errors, that I should otherwise have done."

Wilkinson's official written orders to Pike were dated June 24, 1806, and were artfully worded to provide a legitimate cover for the mission's more dubious purposes. First, Wilkinson charged Pike with the safe return to their home villages of 51 Osage prisoners of war, taken by the Potawatomi and ransomed by the U.S. government for the purposes of improving its relationship with the Osage, whose friendship it valued as essential to the fur trade and as a wedge against the Spanish. "The safe delivery of this charge," Wilkinson stated for the record, "constitutes the primary object of your expedition." That accomplished, Pike was to attempt to mediate a peace between the Osage and the Kansas Indians, toward which end he was to "effect a meeting between the head chiefs of those nations." Next, he was to make peace between the Comanche and tribes inhabiting the land between St. Louis and Comanche territory, notably the Osage, Kansas, and Pawnee. The most skilled horsemen and the fiercest fighters on the prairie, the Comanche were cultivated by both Spain and the United States. As his "interview" with the Comanche was likely to bring him close to the Spanish territory of New Mexico, Wilkinson advised Pike, "it will be necessary you should move with great circumspection . . . to prevent alarm and offense; because the affairs of Spain and the United States appear to be on the point of amicable adjustment." (A letter written by Wilkinson to Dearborn several months earlier provides keener insight into his actual state of mind regarding Spain. In it, he lays out detailed plans for an invasion of the Spanish Southwest and a march on Santa Fe.) Finally, the lieutenant was to complete a survey of the Red and Arkansas rivers. Throughout "the course of your tour," Wilkinson wrote, "you are to remark particularly upon the geographical structure, the natural history, and population of the country through which you may pass, taking care to collect and preserve specimens of everything curious in the mineral or botanical worlds, which can be preserved and are portable."

Wilkinson's written words certainly contained nothing objectionable, but as Pike's subsequent behavior would indicate, he either had an unspoken agreement with the general about the mission's objectives, acted completely beyond his authorization, or was a spectacularly inept geographer. Among other evidence, certain oddities in the composition of the expedition's personnel roster suggest that the first explanation is the most plausible. (He was also inept, but his incompetence is a secondary, not primary, explanation.) Along with the 20 soldiers Pike was assigned, 18 of whom had served under him on the Mississippi expedition, he was persuaded, apparently without protest, to take with him one John Hamilton Robinson, a civilian friend of Wilkinson's, about 24 years of age, who was by training a surgeon. Robinson's purpose on the mission was not primarily to attend to medical needs, however. He had been sent to ensure that even if Pike was unsuccessful in the spying portion of his mission, Wilkinson would obtain some information about Spanish strength in the Southwest. At a certain point in the expedition, Robinson was to detach himself from the main party and proceed alone to Santa Fe, ostensibly to collect

General James Wilkinson, Pike's patron and commanding officer, was one of the most notorious schemers in American history. Donald Jackson, the foremost Pike scholar, concedes that some found the general to be a "charming gallant" but adds that to characterize him as "profoundly a knave puts the historian in no danger of losing perspective."

a debt owed William Morrison, a St. Louis merchant and yet another friend of Wilkinson's. Two years earlier, Morrison had provided Baptiste La Lande, a veteran frontier trader, with several saddlebags filled with goods and sent him off to Santa Fe in still another attempt to persuade the Spanish to open their territory to American traders. After he was taken into custody by the Spanish, La Lande came to like the friendly señoritas of Santa Fe so much that he decided to stay. Robinson's cover story, when he was taken by the Spanish, was to be that he had come to collect the debt owed Morrison by La Lande for the trade goods. Also on Pike's roster was Joseph Ballinger, a tough frontiersman who had been in cahoots with Wilkinson since 1789. Wilkinson persuaded Pike to enlist his former bagman in the army for the expedition and, at its conclusion, to falsify the documents concerning Ballinger's service so that it would appear that he had already served a full five-year hitch and was thus eligible for discharge. A somewhat curious addition as well, for an expedition ordered to be circumspect regarding Spanish territory, was one Antoine F. Baronet Vasquez, who was brought along to interpret Spanish.

The Pike expedition, consisting of 21 soldiers, 2 civilians, and 50-some Osages, departed St. Louis in two keelboats on July 15, 1806. It was a hot and muggy afternoon, as July afternoons in St. Louis tend to be, giving no indication of the travails that lay ahead for the explorers; and probably few of the men, even those who had endured such hardship in the north country on the previous expedition, reflected that they had again started out very late in the season if they hoped to finish their mission by the onset of winter. There is no evidence to suggest that such a thought had occurred to the expedition's leader. In his defense, it must be said that the undefined nature of his mission must have made planning very difficult, particularly as reliable geographic information about the Southwest, especially the approaches to Santa Fe, was essentially nonexistent. Probably, with an unclear idea of the distance to be covered and the nature of the terrain to be traversed, Pike expected to be back by winter.

Slowed by poor weather and the river's powerful current, through what remained of July the expedition made slow progress westward—less than 20 miles per day—up the Missouri to the Osage River, which merges with the Big Muddy near present-day Jefferson City. For the most part, the Indians preferred to walk along the river's banks; those soldiers not required to tow the boats rode in them. The party stopped frequently at settlements along the way to speak with fur traders, who in the early days of western exploration were often the most reliable sources of geographic information. The stops also allowed Pike to collect mail from Wilkinson, who wished to be kept apprised of the expedition's progress, and to dispatch his responses.

Wilkinson's letters, although always an unreliable gauge of his true state of mind, indicate that he did indeed expect Pike back by winter. The general also expressed concern for his son, Lieutenant James Biddle Wilkinson, who was to lead the Arkansas River survey, asking Pike to gradually accustom the somewhat sickly young man to the hardships of wilderness service. "My Son has the foundation of a good Constitution but it must be tempered by degrees," Wilkinson wrote on July 18. "Do not push him beyond his Capacities in hardship too suddenly. He will I hope attempt any thing but let the stuff be hardened by degrees."

Pike's response, written four days letter, not only reassured Wilkinson about the welfare of his son but indicates that he had indeed reached a secret understanding with his commander concerning the nature of the mission. He advised Wilkinson that his son was faring well and was doing a good job overseeing the Osage, with whom he had been marching on land. He also informed the general that he had hit upon a stratagem for reconnoitering Spanish territory and reaching Santa Fe—he would simply advance into Comanche lands as ordered, which would take him

In his travels, Pike did indeed pass through regions that resembled the classic conception of a desert, most notably the sand dunes on the western side of the Colorado Rockies, but in his writings he classified virtually the entire West—"the vast tract of untimbered country which lies between the waters of the Missouri, Mississippi, and the western ocean, from the mouth of the latter river to the 48[th degree] north latitude"—as essentially uninhabitable wasteland.

into territory claimed by Spain. When confronted by Spanish authorities, he would proclaim innocently that he was lost and, out of "politeness," would offer to visit the appropriate dignitaries in Santa Fe to offer explanations and apologies. This plan, he wrote Wilkinson, "would gratify our most sanguine expectations." He recognized that in carrying it out his party would run the risk of being made prisoners of war, but the prospect did not worry him much; in that case, he said, he would "trust to the magnanimity of our Country for liberation."

A little more than a month after its departure from St. Louis, the expedition arrived at the Osage villages, where the ransomed prisoners were reunited with their loved ones and Pike sought to ensure the Indians of the good intentions of the United States toward them. At Wilkinson's directions, he also arrested three agents of the St. Louis fur trader Manuel Lisa, who was a great rival of the Chouteaus. With good reason, Wilkinson believed that Lisa was

attempting to open up his own trade route to Santa Fe, a goal that the general, using the information that Pike obtained, was determined that only he would accomplish. With his characteristic confusion of national and personal interests, Wilkinson informed Pike, in a letter dated August 6, that "no good can be derived to the United States" from Lisa's scheme.

The expedition remained with the Osage for two weeks. It was extremely well received, so much so that Pike had reason to humorously complain about the great number of feasts he was invited to attend. In his journal and the formal report that he compiled after the completion of the expedition, Pike commented on the "flattering reception" he and his men received at the Osage villages and on the magnificence of the surrounding countryside, which he called "one of the most beautiful the eye ever beheld." Deer, bears, elk, turkeys, pronghorn antelope, and buffalo were abundant, and as both timber and water were plentiful near the home of the Osage, Pike envisioned it as a likely site for future white settlement, waxing sentimental about the "future seats of husbandry, the numerous herds of domestic animals, which are no doubt destined to crown with joy these happy plains." In his inability to see that the Osage, in their own fashion, had already crowned the happy plains with joy, Pike was a typical American of his day. He was clear-sighted enough to record that the Osage "towns hold more people in the same space of ground, than any places I ever saw" and that the "Osage raise large quantities of corn, beans, and pumpkins, which they manage with the greatest economy, in order to make it last from year to year," yet still blind enough to characterize the Indians as savages because they belonged to "those nations purely erratic" who were nomadic and depended on hunting for their subsistence.

These reflections represent an exception to the general drift of Pike's commentary about the flat, essentially treeless land the expedition traversed on much of its journey—

that "vast tract of untimbered country which lies between the waters of the Missouri, Mississippi, and the western Ocean" that is usually referred to as the Great Plains. The land east of the Mississippi was still, for the most part, thickly forested, so heavily wooded that it was said that a squirrel could gambol from the Atlantic Coast to the Great Lakes without touching the ground. Americans had grown accustomed to regarding heavy stands of timber as indicative of the fertility of the land that supported it, and a large supply of wood, which was of course the primary building material of the day, was regarded as essential to successful long-term settlement. As there was nothing east of the Mississippi to compare with the seemingly endless rolling prairies of the Great Plains, which Pike was among the first Americans to see, he should not be faulted too severely for characterizing the West as being poorly suited for settlement. The plains, he wrote, were little more than a great barren tract, "parched and dried up for eight months in the year. . . . These vast plains of the western hemisphere may become in time equally celebrated as the sandy desarts of Africa; for I saw in my route, in various places, tracts of many leagues, where the wind had thrown up the sand, in all the fanciful forms of the ocean's rolling wave, and on which not a speck of vegetable matter existed."

Thus was born the belief that much of the West constituted the Great American Desert, an arid region unsuited for agriculture and thus unfit for extensive American settlement. This view was reinforced by subsequent American explorers of the West and the Southwest, most notably Major Stephen Long. Ironically, Pike saw the West's desolation as a benefit to the United States, as the "immense prairies" would limit the westward movement of its citizens, otherwise "so prone to rambling and extending themselves, on the frontiers" to the "borders of the Missouri and Mississippi." This, in Pike's eyes, would strengthen the union, and the prairies would serve as a buffer against

foreign attack. They could also be used as a sort of natural preserve for the Indians. Pike foresaw only that "the prairies incapable of cultivation" would be left "to the wandering and uncivilized" Indian nations already living there, who "as they depend solely on the chase for subsistence[,] . . . require large tracts of country," but beginning in the 1830s the federal government would use the plains as relocation sites for eastern tribes whose native lands were desired by white settlers.

On September 1, Pike set out across the Great Plains for the Pawnee villages located along the Republican River near the present-day border between Kansas and Nebraska. More than 30 Indians, including 4 Pawnees who had been visiting the Osage, traveled with his party, which now crossed the rolling prairies on horses, purchased at what the whites regarded as extortionate prices from the Osage's vast herd. At the Pawnee villages, Pike hoped to mediate a peace between the Osage and their traditional enemy, the Kansas. Warring Indians were bad for trade, and they tended to frighten off potential settlers; many of the early

American soldiers listen as a Pawnee chief makes his point. Seen here is Seymour's portrayal of Long's council with the Pawnee, the first artistic depiction of such a meeting between government emissaries and the Pawnee. At Pike's council with the Pawnee, some 13 years earlier, the Indians acknowledged the American pretension to sovereignty in the region but were clearly more concerned with maintaining good relations with the Spanish.

Seymour was also the first to depict the Kansas Indians, some of whom he has drawn here dancing a tribal ceremony. Pike did not visit the Kansas villages, but a few Kansas did attend his council at the Pawnee settlements, although none could be persuaded to visit St. Louis, as Wilkinson wished them to do.

government explorers of the West, such as Lewis and Clark, were charged with similar diplomatic missions. As the Pawnee maintained tolerably good relations with both the Osage and the Kansas, their villages were to serve as a sort of neutral site for the peace conference, which Pike hoped that some representatives of the Comanche would also attend. All the assembled Indians would then be made aware that the United States now held sovereignty over the region, and they would be strongly encouraged to break off relations with the Spanish traders to the southwest in favor of the American newcomers.

Although the Pawnee villages were to the northwest of the Osage settlements, Pike, at the behest of his Osage guide, initially led his party slightly southwest, along the Little Osage River and then across the Neosho River before veering northward across the Neosho again and then across the Smoky Hill River. The Osage wished to skirt those lands claimed by the Kansas, of whom they were greatly respectful, if not outrightly afraid. (Though "a small nation," Pike wrote, the Kansas were "yet more brave than their Osage brethren, being although not more than one third their number their most dreaded enemies, and frequently making the Pawnees tremble.") The strangeness of the topography and the men's complaint of "blistered and very sore feet" notwithstanding, it was not particularly hard going, and the hunting was outstanding. The plains so teemed with wildlife that nearly every day Pike recorded the success of the expedition's hunters in his journal—"Killed one deer. . . . Killed six buffalo, one elk, and three deer"—and on at least one occasion he cautioned his troops, who had grown overexuberant in their sport, to shoot only what the party needed for food, citing moral qualms about the wanton slaughter of God's creatures. He had less success restraining the Osage, who killed as many buffalo as they could to sabotage their enemy's autumn hunt. Pike wrote that there were so many animals on the prairie that a single hunter could easily support 200 men. Aside from the balkiness of the Osage, who began to drift homeward in groups of two and three as the party advanced, the greatest obstacle to the expedition's progress

The Comanche were the most feared warriors and the best horsemen of the lower plains. Pike had orders "to effect an interview and establish a good understanding" with the Comanche, but he never met with them.

The Pawnee move to their winter settlement. Pike was not as impressed by the Pawnee as he was by the Osage; he referred to their "degeneracy of manners" and stated that they "were neither so brave nor honest as their more northern neighbors." The Pawnee's cowardice and dishonesty apparently consisted mainly in their resistance to his plans.

was the torrential rains they encountered in mid-September. On days when the downpour was too severe for the party to move forward, Pike whiled away the hours in his tent reading the Bible and the essays of Alexander Pope; one day, he amused himself by joining the enlisted men for a comradely round of tattooing.

The conference at the Pawnee villages proved a failure, even though, in his own words, Pike "effected a meeting . . . between a few Kans[as] and Osages, who smoked the pipe of peace and buried the hatchet," significant more in that it represented the first penetration of an official

U.S. delegation to this portion of the Great Plains than for any lasting diplomatic triumph. The Comanche could not be convinced to attend, and Pike was disconcerted to learn that a massive Spanish military force, numbering several hundred men and many more pack animals, had been to the villages just ahead of him, intent on concluding a treaty with the Pawnee and the Kansas and, in Pike's words, on "striking a dread into those different nations of the Spanish power." The Spanish force had made "a great impression on the minds of the young men," according to Pike.

Indeed, the flag of Spain was flying outside the main chief's lodge when Pike and his men arrived at the village on September 25. The conference took place four days later, attended by some Kansas and Osage but mainly by Pawnee; Pike, in his address to the assembled Indians, sought to impress upon them "that they must either be the children of the Spaniards or acknowledge their American father. . . . after next year we will not permit Spanish officers, or soldiers, to come into this country." His oration at last convinced a Pawnee elder to replace the Spanish flag with an American one that Pike gave him, but the American lieutenant recognized that the Indian acted less out of conviction than expediency; his was a triumph of immediacy, not power. The Spanish had been visiting the Pawnee for a lot longer than the Americans had; one need only look at the size of their respective delegations to judge their power in the region. Caught between two powerful nations, both of whom wished to use the Indians to advance their own interests, which were diametrically opposed, the Pawnee (and other tribes, at other places and times) attempted to placate both. The Americans were there now, so the American flag would fly, but Pike wrote that as the Stars and Stripes climbed the pole outside the chief's lodge, "every face in the council was clouded with sorrow, as if some great national calamity was about to befal them."

Lost in the Mountains

Pike soon had further evidence that the Indians were still concerned with the Spanish force that had passed through their territory. On October 1, as Pike was preparing to march his troops southward to the Arkansas River, he learned from White Wolf, the Pawnee chief, that the Spanish had been in the area, in part, to intercept the American expedition. (The Spanish authorities in the Southwest had been tipped off about Pike either by spies or Wilkinson himself. The general was in a bit of trouble: He had lost his governorship because of complaints about his corruption, he was in hot water with Dearborn for resisting the secretary's orders to move against Spanish provocations along the Sabine River, and rumors about the Burr plot were circulating everywhere, it seemed. If Wilkinson did betray Pike, he could have done so for several reasons. Many historians believe that Wilkinson, realizing that his plans with Burr were about to come to light, had decided by this point to betray Burr himself in an attempt to save his own skin. With his situation in the United States rapidly deteriorating, Wilkinson was very concerned with maintaining his options with Spain, the argument goes, so he then betrayed Pike as well, presenting him and his men, as it were, to the Spanish authorities as living proof of his continued good intentions. If Wilkinson had not firmly decided to bail out of his scheme with Burr, he still

Western explorers at their riverside encampment roast their dinner—a buffalo hump and several of its ribs. Pike and his men supped on such repasts on many nights.

might have betrayed Pike, in the belief that a border con-
frontation between American and Spanish forces would
have furthered his aim of a war between the two nations.)

In any event, once Pike revealed his plans to White
Wolf, the Indian used everything in his power, including
the threat of force, to persuade him to go no farther and
return to St. Louis. The Spanish had wished to venture
farther eastward, the chief told Pike, into indisputably
American territory, but they had heeded the Pawnee's
entreaties and retreated south. He asked that the Americans be as respectful of their new friends' wishes—"he
therefore hoped we would be equally reasonable" was how
Pike put it—but when the lieutenant insisted that his party
was going to move south, White Wolf explained that the
Pawnee had promised the Spanish that they would halt
the American advance, by armed force if necessary. The
Pawnee should do what they must, Pike replied, but they
should understand that the "young warriors of the great
American father were not women to be turned back by
words." He recognized that the Pawnee warriors far out-
numbered his small band, he said, but even if the Indians
should triumph now, more troops would come, in greater
numbers, and exact a terrible revenge. A tense standoff
ensued. All that night, as the soldiers attempted to sleep
in their encampment, Pawnee warriors rode by, whooping
and screaming, in an attempt to unnerve the Americans.
Sentries fired upon the riders several times, but no one
was injured; after several days, the evident determination
of the Americans to fight, if necessary, convinced the
Indians to relent, and on October 7 the expedition departed
the region of the Pawnee villages without bloodshed.

Pike marched his men south across the endless prairies
along the flattened trail through the grasslands made by
the passage of the huge Spanish force. He had now come
to regard the presence of the Spanish troops, so long as
he could avoid an encounter, as a blessing of fortune, for
he believed that by following the Spanish trail he could

discover the easiest route to Santa Fe. The prospect made him optimistic about attaining the most important objective of his mission. Before leaving the Pawnee villages, he wrote Wilkinson that "any number of men (who may reasonably be calculated on) would find no difficulty in marching the same route we came with baggage wagons, field artillery, and all the usual appendages of a small army; and if all the route to Santa Fe should be of the same description in case of war, I would pledge my life (and what is infinitely dearer, my honor) for the successful march of a reasonable body of troops into the province of New Mexico."

Pike reached the Arkansas on October 18, a few days after the main body of the expedition. The great swaths that the migrating herds of buffalo cut through the prairie had obliterated the Spanish trail, and Pike and Dr. Robinson detached themselves from the rest of the party to search for it while the younger Wilkinson led the remainder of the men on to the Arkansas. When torrential rains further obliterated any markings on the prairie, the two searchers themselves became lost. Pike later described their "situation" as "not the most agreeable, not having more than four rounds of ammunition each, and 400 miles in the nearest direction from the first civilized inhabitant," but after a couple of days they were found and led to the camp Wilkinson had established on the Arkansas.

There, after 10 days and the disagreements detailed by the younger Wilkinson in his letters to Pike and his father, the party split up. Wilkinson's party, in their leaky canoes, which had to be repaired after just 100 yards of sailing, headed down the Arkansas to the Mississippi, which it reached after a journey of 73 days that left the lieutenant sick and exhausted. Pike and his men headed west, following the Arkansas and the rediscovered trail of the Spanish soldiers toward the mountains that lay, no one knew quite for sure how many miles away, to the west. Snow fell regularly as the small party made its way along the

Prairie dogs and their burrows fascinated the first American explorers of the West. Pike encountered large numbers of the playful, short-tailed, herbivorous rodents with the barking call near and along the Arkansas River. He discovered them to be "excellent meat, after they were exposed a night or two to the frost, by which means the rankness acquired by their subterraneous dwelling is corrected."

river from present-day Kansas into Colorado, but the explorers as yet endured no great hardship. Vast herds of elks, antelope, and buffalo, often pursued by wolves and coyotes, shared the plains with them; at one point Pike reported that "the face of the prairie was covered with [buffalo] . . . their numbers exceeded the imagination." On another day, the expedition encountered a herd of mustangs, the wild descendants of the horses brought by the original Spanish settlers of the Southwest to the New World. (The horse is not native to North America; even the horses belonging to the various Plains Indians tribes were descended from those originally brought by the Spanish.) Pike wrote that "when within a quarter of a mile, they discovered us, and came immediately up near us, making the earth tremble under them . . . [like] a charge of cavalry. They stopt and gave us an opportunity to view them, among them were some very beautiful bays, blacks and greys, and indeed of all colors." The mustangs were too wily and swift to permit capture, however, despite the best efforts of Pike's men. Other animals proved easier to bag, and Pike reported that the company "feasted sumptiously" on meat obtained by its hunters. Normally, the company's best marksmen were designated for the hunting detail.

By November 11, when the expedition crossed into Colorado, conditions were worsening. Nighttime temperatures consistently plunged below freezing, and the men, who had not been equipped for winter, began to complain of the cold. Game was growing scarcer, and the expedition's horses were tiring from overwork; two of them had to be left for dead. Although Pike recognized "the impossibility of performing the voyage in the time proposed," that is, before winter, he was, he wrote, "determined to spare no pains to accomplish every object even should it oblige me to spend another winter in the desert."

On the afternoon of November 15, Pike, with the aid of a spyglass, spotted ahead of him, looking "like a small

A detail from an engraved facsimile of Seymour's Distant View of the Rocky Mountains. *Pike first glimpsed the Rockies on November 15, 1806, looming on the horizon "like a small blue cloud." In one of his less expansionist moments, he was later to propose the Rockies, which he called the Mexican Mountains, as a natural boundary between the United States and New Spain.*

blue cloud," what he determined to be a mountain range. He was looking upon the Front Range, the easternmost of the Colorado Rockies. His men "with one accord gave three cheers to the Mexican mountains," presumably because with their appearance the end of the outward leg of their journey, at least figuratively speaking, was also in sight.

But the most hellish portion of their trek was just beginning. Deceived by the flatness of the terrain and the clearness of the air, Pike had supposed the range to be at most a few days' march away, but it took his weary band a week to travel the 100 miles that separated it from them. En route, another horse died, and the party enjoyed its last successful hunting for a while. Seventeen buffalo were killed, furnishing a "general feast of [136] marrow bones" and 900 pounds of meat. The meat, which was dried for transport, would certainly be welcome, but it was a difficult burden for a group that was beginning to run short of pack animals. Then, in the shadow of the flinty peaks, the expedition was waylaid by a war party of 60 Pawnees, made more belligerent than usual by their failure to locate any Comanche. As Pike put it, "An unsuccessful war party . . . are always ready to embrace an opportunity, of gratifying their disappointed vengeance, on the first persons whom they meet." With extreme difficulty, Pike persuaded the Indians to smoke a peace pipe with him, but the Pawnee, insulted at the quality of the gifts offered by the whites—tobacco, knives, and flints; they preferred ammunition, food, iron kettles, and blankets—swarmed around the soldiers and began helping themselves to goods. Through threats and bluster, Pike at last succeeded in driving them off, but he felt himself grievously insulted "that the smallness of my number obliged me thus to submit to the insults of a lawless banditti, it being the first time a savage took any thing from me."

Pike's behavior, which was often puzzling, was soon to grow inexplicable. Believing himself to be near the source

At a little more than 14,000 feet in height, Pikes Peak towers over its immediate neighbors in the Front Range, one of the easternmost chains of the Rocky Mountains. Pike, who aspired to the mountain's summit, proved unable to surmount even the lower surrounding peaks.

of the Arkansas, or so he later professed, he ordered his men to erect a small fortress near the river. Then, while his men maintained this "defensible position" near the junction of the Arkansas and Fountain Creek (the site of present-day Pueblo, Colorado), he, Robinson, and privates Theodore Miller and John Brown set out to climb a towering "blue mountain" that loomed an afternoon's march (Pike's estimate) to the northwest, ostensibly so that the lieutenant could get the lay of the land from the mountain's summit. Two days of arduous "climbing over many small hills covered with cedars and pitch pines" brought the adventurers to what they believed to be the base of Grand Peak, as Pike termed it. On November 26, the four men, carrying no provisions, clad only in light cotton overalls and wearing no socks under their worn moccasins, began their ascent, fully confident of reaching the top and returning to their base camp that same day. Four days later, frozen, "hungry, dry, and extremely sore," defeated by "rocks almost perpendicular," they gave up, having succeeded only in climbing a much smaller peak, probably Cheyenne Mountain. Pikes Peak, the misnomer by which the lieutenant's blue mountain is known today, stood unbested still some 15 miles off, "as high again," according to Pike, "as what we had ascended," so icy and rugged "that no human being could have ascended to its pinical."

After returning to the rude stockade on the Arkansas, Pike led his men west along the river and into the mountains. In an October 24 letter to Wilkinson, he had stated that he intended to follow the Arkansas only until he reached the mountains, at which point he would head south in search of the Red River. Somewhere along the line he had changed his mind; he apparently believed that he was still following the path made by the Spanish force, but he was in fact on an old Indian trail that would lead him away from Santa Fe. Winter had now arrived with a vengeance; a furious blizzard halted their progress on December 1, a day on which the temperature dove to 17 degrees below zero. In their inadequate clothing, the men

(continued on page 81)

Under Western Skies

Frederic Remington's Unknown Explorers *traverse a sun-baked canyon in the Southwest. Remington, perhaps the most well known Western artist, visited the Southwest in the 1880s.*

No artists accompanied Zebulon Pike and his men as they made their tortuous way across the rolling plains and snow-capped mountains to the Southwest, for the good reason that spying, rather than science, was the expedition's primary purpose. Before the advent of photography, artists often traveled with expeditions of exploration as members of the scientific team, responsible for creating an accurate visual record of the landscape and its human and animal inhabitants. But Pike's was essentially a military mission, hastily conceived in the utmost secrecy and concerned more with the gathering of intelligence for military and economic purposes than with true exploration. Thus, no firsthand visual documentation of the Pike expedition exists, but those, artists among them, who figuratively followed his trail to the Southwest in succeeding decades found it—with its seemingly endless horizons, its cracked deserts and thirsty canyons, its strange plant life and weird geologic formations, its magnificent mountains—a land of eerie, unsettling beauty.

Chain of Spires Along the Gila River *by John Mix Stanley, who as the artist for Colonel Stephen Watts Kearney's Army of the West during its conquest of New Mexico and subsequent march to the Pacific became the first American painter to portray this region of the Southwest. This painting is more accurate as a romanticized depiction rather than a scientific portrayal, however, for Stanley has brought together in this work exotic plant specimens and unusual topographical features found throughout the Southwest rather than at any specific site on the Gila.*

Samuel Seymour's View of James Peak in the Rain. *Seymour was one of the artists on Major Stephen Long's 1819 expedition to the Colorado Rockies, which was the first official U.S. exploratory mission to the region since Pike's. This pen-and-ink watercolor wash drawing is the first artistic portrayal of Pikes Peak. Note the vegetation in the foreground and the thunderstorm that broke over the Rockies as Seymour was sketching, which represent his subtle commentary on the notion of the region being the Great American Desert.*

Titian Peale, then just 19 years old but the scion of a famous Philadelphia artistic and scientific family, was employed by the Long expedition to draw scientifically accurate portrayals of the animal life it encountered. Here, a prairie wolf dines on an antelope.

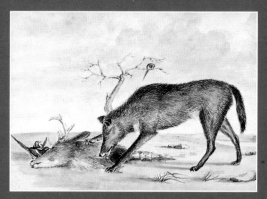

Peale's depiction of a wildfowl encountered by the Long expedition. Peale followed his orders to the letter and did not include any of the surrounding landscape in his portrayals.

The low-slung adobe city of Santa Fe as it
appeared in 1866, by which time it had been in
American hands for 20 years. A seat of
government since its founding in 1609, Santa Fe
is the oldest capital city in the United States.

Fur trappers at work. As Americans began arriving in New Mexico in larger numbers in the 1820s, they discovered that the streams, creeks, and rivers in the southern reaches of the Rocky Mountains were still rich in fur-bearing animals, especially the beaver. The mountain men operating out of the New Mexico settlement of Taos were among the first of the so-called free trappers.

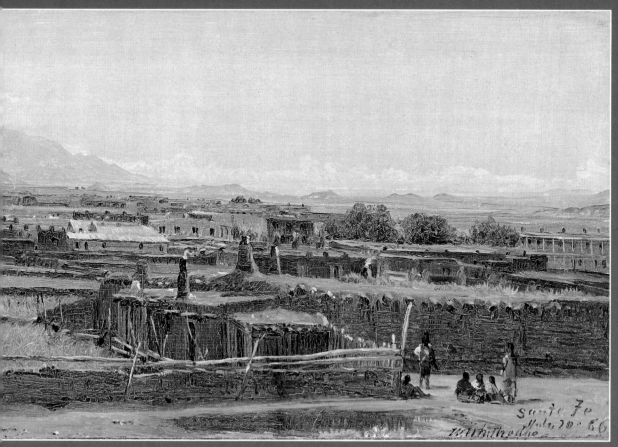

Lieutenant George Brewertons' Jornada del Muerto, or Journey of Death. Painted in 1853, a time when increasing numbers of emigrants were making the perilous overland journey through the Great American Desert to fertile California, Brewerton's work captures the terror that the barren wastes west of the Great Salt Lake held for the pioneers.

(continued from page 72)

suffered greatly, but their tribulations were not as severe as those undergone by the horses, which had grown weak and emaciated. In vain the beasts attempted to forage beneath the steadily accumulating snow, "and to increase their misfortunes," as Pike wrote, "the poor animals were attacked by the magpies, who attracted by the scent of their sore backs, alighted on them, and in defiance of their wincing and kicking, picked many places quite raw." Pike claimed that these scavenger birds had grown so bold as to grab meat right from his men's hands. The next day, impassable cliffs forced the party to ford the icy Arkansas, as a result of which two of the men contracted frostbite in their feet. Driven mad by its suffering, one of the horses simply ran off into the frozen ravines, whinnying in agony.

On December 5, the expedition camped near the site of present-day Canon City, Colorado, near the narrow chasm on the river known today as Royal Gorge. There were buffalo in the area, and while Pike pondered his next move, his men fashioned crude shelters, blankets and wraps, and a kind of moccasin from the skins of the shaggy ruminants. After four days of rest and recovery, Pike ordered his men north, along yet another Indian trail that he believed had been made by the Spanish. Both Santa Fe and the Red River lay in the opposite direction; Pike convinced himself that the trail would eventually wind south.

So this most curious of exploring expeditions moved northward, away from its stated and unstated objectives, deep into the heart of the greatest mountain range on the continent in the dead of winter. Snow fell constantly; the men shivered and cursed; the horses bruised their hooves on the frosty trail; occasionally one lay down and died. On December 11, Pike and his men camped near present-day Cripple Creek, Colorado; two days later, they came to another river, which Pike correctly ascertained was the South Platte. This deduction aside, he possessed not the remotest idea of where he was or where he was going, "as the geography of the country turned out to be so different

A discouraged Pike and his companions survey Pikes Peak from a ridge on Cheyenne Mountain. Ridiculously unprepared for the ordeal ahead of them, Pike and his men started up what they believed to be Pikes Peak on the morning of November 26, confidently expecting to reach the summit that afternoon.

Pike's ignorance of western geography, which was no greater than anyone else's at the time, does not excuse his decision to lead his expedition into the Rocky Mountains in the dead of winter. Only the greatest of good fortune prevented any of his men from dying, and several were left permanently disabled by their ordeal.

from our expectations." Meanwhile, as Pike put it, his "poor fellows suffered extremely from the cold," and the horses continued to waste away, sicken, and die. Still, he continued north, and then northwest. Near present-day Buena Vista, another river was encountered. Pike, inexplicably, believed it at first to be the Red (he knew all along that the Red lay well to the south), but it was in fact the northern branch of the Arkansas. Taking with him 2 men, Pike marched 25 miles northward along the river's course, until he had satisfied himself that he had reached its source, then with the entire party trekked southeastward downriver. Christmas was especially grim; although there was still plenty of buffalo meat, the men were cold, frustrated, and most likely growing impatient with their commander's blundering. Most no longer had any blankets, having been forced to cut them up to make socks and wraps for their bloody and frozen feet.

The New Year brought no end to their ordeal. The meat had run out, and malnutrition was becoming a problem. The horses skidded and fell off the icy, twisting trail. Pike had to shoot one; two more went insane and bolted. Although Pike did not yet realize it, the expedition was now approaching the other end of Royal Gorge. The passage through the chasm was particularly arduous, requiring the men to resort at times to the use of crudely fashioned wooden sleds to move along frozen sections of the river and at other points to scale the sheer canyon walls to bypass turbulent regions where the river still raged. And once out of the gorge, Pike and his men experienced a sickening moment of recognition. In the distance, "the unbounded space of the prairies again presented themselves," and Pike recognized, "with great mortification," that for the past month he had been tracing a huge circle. The expedition had arrived once more at the Canon City campsite where it had stopped on December 5.

As winter deepened and Pike's bewilderment grew, starvation and exposure became increasingly greater threats to the safety of his men.

A MAP
of
THE INTERNAL PROVINCES
of
NEW SPAIN.

The Outlines are from the Sketches of his corrected and improved by Captain ZEBULON M. PIKE, who was conducted through that COUNTRY, in the Year 1807 by Order of the Commandant General of those Provinces.

REFERENCES.

Division of Maps
MAY 4 1931
Library of Congress

GULF OF MEXICO

Is This Not the Red River?

Pike rarely let slip his veneer of supreme self-confidence, but in his journal he felt compelled to confess that by this point he was "at a considerable loss how to proceed." His men were starving, ill, and unhappy; his pack animals were exhausted to the point of uselessness; there were still several months of winter remaining. The most logical thing to do was to follow the Arkansas eastward, back the way he had come, and either return to St. Louis or find a more suitable spot for a winter encampment. Instead, after "mature deliberation," he decided to leave two men— Patrick Smith and Antoine Vasquez—on the spot with all the horses and remaining supplies, while the rest of the expedition crossed the mountains on foot in search of the Red River. A small party would then be sent back to escort the by then presumably refreshed animals and the two men over the mountains.

Staggering under the weight of the 70-pound pack they were each made to carry, the men made their way south-west into the rugged Sangre de Cristo Mountains (a range of the Rockies that stretches southward from southern Colorado into central New Mexico), fighting their way through tremendous drifts of snow in temperatures that ranged between 0 and 18 below, for the first four days without any food. On the morning of January 18, Pike and Robinson, who were the only two strong enough for the task, went out hunting. After spotting a small herd of

Pike's map of the internal provinces of New Spain, which was based on the famous Prussian geographer Alexander von Humboldt's map of the same region. When Humboldt complained to Jefferson that Pike and the British cartographer Aaron Arrowsmith had made unauthorized use of his map, Jefferson asked the Prussian to forgive Pike because he had done so "on a principle of enlarging knowledge and not for filthy shillings and pence." The Englishman's theft, Jefferson added, "was in the piratical spirit of his country."

buffalo, they crawled a mile in the snow to position them-selves for a shot. They succeeded in wounding two buffalo, but the powerful creatures lumbered off with the rest of the herd, leaving the pair of disconsolate and desperate explorers "determined to remain absent and die by our-selves rather than to return to our camp and behold the misery of our poor lads." Fortunately, they soon spotted another creature, which they dropped with one shot. A drink of the animal's blood gave them enough strength to butcher the beast and stumble back to camp with some meat.

But no sooner was one crisis resolved than another arose. More than half of the party was suffering from frostbite and frozen joints, and two men, John Sparks and Thomas Daugherty, soon found that they could no longer continue. On January 22, Pike made the heart-wrenching decision to abandon them. Leaving "the two poor lads who were to remain with ammunition," Pike "made use of every argument in my power to encourage them to have fortitude to resist their fate; and gave them assurance of sending relief as soon as possible." Then, "not without tears," the expedition pressed on. Three more days of hunger ensued before another buffalo was killed; the dis-content among the ranks had now grown so pronounced that to restore order Pike had to threaten to shoot a mu-tineer, John Brown, who had dared express his opinion that "it was more than human nature could bear, to march three days without sustenance, through snows three feet deep, and carry burthens only fit for horses." (The quoted language is Pike's; it may be inferred that Brown's objec-tions were actually expressed a good deal more forcefully.) On January 27, Henry Menaugh had to be left behind, but that night the expedition made camp on a westward running body of water that Pike took to be at last the headwaters of the Red River. It was not, but by following its path out of the mountains and along the edges of a stretch of massive sand dunes, hundreds of feet high, the weary band was brought into the San Luis Valley, which offered them a welcome respite from the travail of the mountains. (The body of water was Mendano Creek; the region of sand dunes—one part of Pike's Southwest that truly is desertlike—is known today as Great Sand Dunes National Monument.) There, from a hilltop, Pike spied yet another river. This time, he was certain, he had reached the Red River. After proceeding downstream for several miles and satisfying himself that he had at last found the headwaters of that elusive watercourse, Pike, on the final day of January 1807, at last called a halt.

He spent the next month in a cottonwood stockade that his men constructed on a western tributary (the Rio Conejos) of the river he believed to be the Red, accompanied for much of that time by only four of his comrades. The edifice was well constructed for defense; 36 feet square, it was surrounded by a breastwork of sharpened stakes and a water-filled moat and could be entered only by crawling over a retractable plank. Armed with the somewhat spurious pretext, as Pike himself admitted, of Morrison's debt, Robinson went on ahead to see if he could make his way to Santa Fe, while Pike deputed Corporal Jeremiah Jackson and four men to go back into the mountains to see if they could rescue the stragglers. It was heroic service that Pike was asking, particularly of soldiers so hard used, and his men responded courageously; in the end, the men that he so dismissively characterized as a "damn'd set of rascals" certainly owed their survival as much to their own strength and courage as to their commander's astuteness.

On February 16, a Spanish dragoon appeared at the fort and informed Pike that Robinson had arrived in Santa Fe; the American told his Spanish counterpart that he would be happy to pay a visit to Señor Alencaster, the Spanish governor of New Mexico, if that gentleman so desired. The next morning, Jackson arrived with two men and told Pike that Menaugh was on the way with the others. He also had a less pleasant message. Sparks and Daugherty

Pike and his bedraggled men are led into Santa Fe by a Spanish patrol. This version of the event was painted many years after the fact by Frederic Remington, perhaps the most well known artist of the West. According to Pike, the Spanish were astonished by the ragged appearance of the Americans.

were still unfit to travel; their condition had so worsened that they had given Jackson the bones from their frozen and gangrenous toes, which had fallen off from exposure, to present to their commander as a grim entreaty, "by all that was sacred, not to leave them to perish far from the civilized world." The accusation that he would abandon two of his "poor lads" stung Pike to the marrow. "Ah! little did they know my heart, if they could suspect me of conduct so ungenerous," he wrote. "No! before they should be left, I would for months have carried the end of a litter, in order to secure them the happiness of once more seeing their native homes." Two days later, Corporal William Meek and Theodore Miller volunteered to hike the almost 200 miles back to where Smith and Vasquez were camped on the Arkansas, retrieve the two men and the horses, and rescue Sparks and Daugherty. Pike, to his credit, duly noted their heroism in his journal.

One hundred Spanish soldiers, commanded by Bartholomew Fernandez, arrived at the fortress on February 26. In a cordial tone, Fernandez diplomatically informed Pike, through an interpreter, that Governor Alencaster understood that he was lost. He, Fernandez, was authorized to offer the Americans whatever they needed—horses, food, money, ammunition, as well as an armed escort—to reach the headwaters of the Red River, which was eight days' journey from Santa Fe, where the Americans would be taken first. "What? Is this not the Red River?" Pike exclaimed, only to learn that he was encamped within Spanish territory on the Rio Grande.

Historians still debate Pike's sincerity in uttering that question. It is argued that surely he could not have seriously believed that he was anywhere near the Red, which is hundreds of miles to the south and flows west to east, rather than north to south, as does the Rio Grande at that point. Adherents of this viewpoint cite Wilkinson's evident desire that Pike reconnoiter Spanish territory and the evidence of Pike's willingness to do so, including his written intention to claim that he was lost should he be challenged

In the mountains surrounding Santa Fe—the Sandia Range to the south, the Sangre de Cristo chain to the east, and the Jemez Mountains to the south—gold and silver were mined. The New Mexicans were willing to pay in precious metals for manufactured goods, which is one reason why American entrepreneurs were so eager to open a trade route to Santa Fe.

by the Spanish. And at least one member of Pike's party subsequently claimed that Pike and all his men knew that they were on the Rio Grande.

On the other hand, as Donald Jackson, the foremost scholar of the Pike expedition, has pointed out, if Pike was not confused about his whereabouts on February 26, he most certainly had been not long before. There can be no doubt that Pike had been badly lost while in the mountains. To state that he was careless, foolhardy, self-seeking, and unforgivably reckless with his men's well-being in challenging the Rockies in wintertime is undoubtedly accurate, but to imply that he blundered about the mountains on purpose, as a pretext to fool the Spanish, is to impute to him a sinister nature that few of even his harshest critics would credit. Most likely, Pike went into the mountains believing that in so doing he would find a route to Santa Fe or the Red River's headwaters and then became lost. (This latter notion is not inconceivable when one considers how little geographic information on the West in general, and on the Southwest in particular, was available. For example, Pike, in his travels up the Arkansas, claimed to have found the headwaters of the river later known as the Yellowstone, which is in actuality more than 500 miles north of the northernmost point Pike reached. Yet the notion that the Yellowstone was only a short portage from southern rivers such as the Colorado and the Arkansas persisted for decades. At the time Pike set out, many geographic authorities, including the estimable Prussian explorer Alexander von Humboldt, whose map of the Southwest was the most comprehensive in existence, placed the Red's headwaters in the Rockies.) When the Spanish troops found Pike in his fortress on the Rio Conejos near the Rio Grande, he may or may not have known that he was not on the Red River, he almost certainly knew that he was near if not in Spanish territory (otherwise, why send Robinson on ahead?), and he probably was, to a certain extent, lost, which is not to say that he was not engaged on a spying mission. In other words, the fiction

Like La Mesilla, portrayed here, most New Mexico towns were built around a large, open central square, called a plaza, where the church and possibly government and other official buildings were likely to stand. The great majority of buildings were long, low structures made of adobe—sun-dried brick.

Pike had concocted as a pretense for the spying mission had become a reality.

After leaving a small force behind to await the arrival of the Americans still in the mountains, the Spanish took Pike and the rest of his men as "guests" to Santa Fe and then on to Chihuahua in Mexico via the famed Camino Real, or King's Highway, the road that connected the far-flung reaches of Spain's colonial empire. Although he was questioned several times about the nature of his mission, Pike always maintained his story that he had possessed no greater designs than to survey the Red River and had become lost, which Wilkinson's carefully worded written orders seemed to verify. For the most part, he and his men were treated with extreme courtesy and were allowed to keep their weapons and uniforms, such as they were— Pike reported his "mortification" at appearing before the refined denizens of Santa Fe clad in ragged blue pants, moccasins, a blanket, and "a cap made of scarlet cloth, lined with fox skins"; each of his men wore leggings, a breechcloth, a leather coat, and no cap, leading the more fashionably clad Spanish to inquire if the Americans lived in tents like Indians. As they proceeded from village to village southward along the Camino Real, Pike made copious notes on the geography, landscape, wildlife, population, government, history, climate, and armed forces of New Spain, which he secreted in the barrels of his men's rifles. He was even able to purchase, as a gift for Jefferson, two grizzly bear cubs, which were carried in a large cage on the back of one of the mules provided for the Americans by the Spanish. At halts in the journey, Pike wrote, the cubs would be let out, and over time they became so docile that they "would play like young puppies with each other & the soldiers."

There were some tense moments. One Nicolas Cole, an expatriate tailor living in Santa Fe, claimed to Alencaster that Robinson and Pike had approached him about the likelihood of the New Mexicans rising in rebellion against Spain should Wilkinson and 40,000 troops invade

In writing about his travels through New Spain, Pike devoted many words to what he regarded as the undue influence of the Catholic church in the region. Pike wrote that "the influence of that tribunal [i.e., the Catholic authorities] is greater in his Catholic majesty's Mexican dominions, than in any Catholic country in Europe, or perhaps in the world." He generally dismissed the Catholic faith as "superstition."

the province. Daugherty, when he was at last brought out of the mountains, told the Spanish authorities that Wilkinson had assured Pike that if he was not back by Christmas, it would be assumed that he had been taken captive by the Spanish and a force of 15,000 to 20,000 troops would be sent to effect his rescue. But Wilkinson was in no position to dispatch a rescue mission—the Burr conspiracy had been blown sky high, and the general was desperately seeking to save his own skin—and one would not have been necessary in any case. On April 27, Pike and his men were told that they should prepare for their departure. The next morning, escorted by a Spanish force led by Facundo Melgares, who had been in command of the huge column whose trail Pike had followed for a while, the Americans departed Chihuahua. It took 63 days for them to cross northern Mexico and the heart of Texas to Natchitoches, an American outpost on the lower Red River. Upon entering the little frontier town, Pike wrote, he cried "All hail . . . the ever sacred name of country, in which is embraced that of kindred friends, and every other tie which is dear to the soul of man." On this rather implausible note ended one of the strangest expeditions in the annals of American exploration.

Blazing Trails

Pike, who so badly craved the adulation accorded heroes, was destined to be disappointed in that regard in the few years remaining to him. He had expected to be lauded in much the same fashion as had Lewis and Clark, but indifference, if not outright contempt, greeted him upon his return. In order to save himself, Wilkinson had become one of Burr's most vociferous accusers, but there were few who did not believe that the general was himself implicated in the treasonous affair, and their outrage extended to Pike, who was denounced as "a parasite of Wilkinson" and his expedition as a "pre-meditated cooperation with Burr." Not even Burr's acquittal, in the fall of 1807, on charges of treason—it was ruled that Burr's plotting did not constitute the overt act required for conviction—lessened the scorn in which Pike was held in many quarters, in part because he refused to publicly disassociate himself from Wilkinson, even when the general was himself tried (and acquitted) for his various malfeasances. (Pike even swore out a deposition attesting to the general's sterling character and defending him from charges pertaining to the expedition.) Congress refused to reward Pike and his men— the "damn'd set of rascals" that had in the end acquitted itself so courageously—with land grants similar to those it had voted to the men of the Corps of Discovery, and, again in contrast with Lewis and Clark, Pike received no

The legendary mountain man and scout Christopher "Kit" Carson first made a name for himself by helping lead Ewing Young's fur-trapping party from Taos to the Spanish mission of San Gabriel, near present-day Los Angeles, in 1829. Carson was among the explorers who followed Pike and helped open the entire Southwest to American influence.

prestigious political appointments. (Congress's seeming in-
gratitude may be attributed to more than the strong air of
disreputability that now hung about the expedition. Jefferson had been careful to inform Congress that he was
dispatching Lewis and Clark, thereby gaining its implicit
support for that expedition, whereas Wilkinson, who had
no authority to dispatch exploring expeditions, had of
course done no such thing; he had not even seen fit to
inform the president about the mission until after the fact
and had then, of necessity to his plans, withheld several
key details from him.) Pike's journal and reports of his
expedition were not well received; they had to be compiled
from the patchy notes he had managed to hide from the
Spanish, who had confiscated his most important documents, and even his publisher conceded that no book "ever
went to press under so many disadvantages." The *Geographical, statistical, and general observations made by
Capt. Z. M. Pike, on the Interior Provinces of New Spain*
(as Pike's official report was unwieldily titled, in part) demonstrated a certain talent of observation, but as Humboldt
put it, "The numerous statistical data, which Mr. Pike has
collected in a country of the language of which he was
ignorant, are for the greater part very inaccurate." Humboldt would also complain that Pike had stolen his famous
map of the Southwest, which he had lent to Jefferson and
Secretary of Treasury Albert Gallatin, and used it as an
uncredited source for his own. (There is an undeniable
similarity between the two maps, as well as evidence sug-
gesting that Burr and Wilkinson, in their mania for information about the Southwest, made an unauthorized
copy of Humboldt's chart, to which Pike would presumably have been given access. In Pike's defense, Donald
Jackson points out that the American's map improves on
Humboldt's concerning Upper Louisiana.)

   Although Pike was able to resume his career, in part
because of the generosity of Jefferson, and even won pro-
motions, he seldom received the assignments he wanted

and complained at having to serve under officers who were "heavy, dull, fat, unenterprising and incapable." His personal life was tinged with tragedy—four of the children he had with Clarissa died in infancy—and when the War of 1812 broke out, Pike, now a general, uttered his famous vow that the nation would hear of his fame or his death. It was the latter that he found, by means of an exploding powder magazine at the Battle of York in April 1813. Wilkinson, largely because of Jefferson's belief in his integrity, was able to continue his dastardly career for some time, but after his disastrous direction of the American campaign against Montreal in the War of 1812, he was finally discharged from the army. He spent the last 10 years of his life engaged in various attempts to extract money from Spain for his supposed services to it. After a short stint as a representative for the American Bible Society, he died in Mexico City on December 28, 1825, probably as a result of complications arising from his late-blooming opium addiction.

Despite its undeniable elements of farce and fiasco, Pike's expedition was important for a number of reasons. Pike was one of the first Americans to explore the Southwest. As such, his report was influential in determining the future course of American settlement of the West; misconceptions and inaccuracies notwithstanding, it was still the most complete work on the Southwest yet published in the United States. As promulgated by Pike, the notion of the Great American Desert now seems to be a greatly overstated misconception—although many historians argue that given the prevailing technologies of Pike's day, his assessment that the plains were unsuitable for large-scale settlement was accurate—but for decades future explorers found little to dispel it, and it informed the pattern of American settlement of the lands west of the Mississippi. Thus, when American settlers first began moving west in large numbers, they looked for routes that would take them over the plains and beyond the Rockies to the

A detail from Charles Willson Peale's portrait of Stephen Long, who with three companions was the first to climb Pikes Peak. Peale's son, Titian, accompanied Long's expedition to the Rockies as its scientific illustrator. Long was among the first Americans to insist that trained scientific professionals accompany government expeditions of exploration.

Samuel Seymour's View of the Rocky Mountains on the Platte 50 Miles from Their Base *illustrates Edwin James's* Account of an Expedition from Pittsburgh to the Rocky Mountains . . . Under Maj. S. H. Long. *James served as the Long expedition's botanist and official chronicler.*

more hospitable lands of California and Oregon. Likewise, when the federal government deemed it necessary to forcibly relocate Indian tribes of the East, they were given lands on the prairie—a development that Pike's report had anticipated, if not explicitly foreseen. Finally, Pike's comments on Santa Fe and the regions of New Spain—particularly on their great need for imported manufactured goods—confirmed the existing belief that there was money to be made in commerce with the Southwest, and in the decades following his death a number of explorers would build on the work that he had begun. Thus, from the work of Pike and his successors was born the abiding U.S. interest in the Southwest that would culminate in the Mexican War and the formal U.S. acquisition of that region.

The first government-sponsored expedition that built upon Pike's work was commanded by Major Stephen Harriman Long, a Dartmouth graduate, former instructor at West Point, and member of the Army Corps of Topographical Engineers (which was destined to play a crucial role in the exploration of the West) who had prepared for his mission by directing a survey of the nation's western defenses from Arkansas to the Falls of St. Anthony (the

Minnesota region that Pike had purchased from the Sioux). Beginning in June 1820, Long led "a curious cavalcade of disgruntled career officers, eccentric scientists, and artist-playboys," in the words of William H. Goetzmann, overland from the site of present-day Council Bluffs, Iowa, along the Platte and the South Platte rivers to the shadow of the Rocky Mountains. There, Long and several of his men climbed the tall mountain that had bedeviled Pike and that would come to bear the earlier explorer's name. In late July, his westward progress deterred by forbidding Royal Gorge, Long divided his party for the return journey east. Despite several desertions and many encounters with Kiowa, Arapaho, and Cheyenne Indians, the group led by Captain John Bell succeeded in descending the Arkansas to present-day Belle Point, Oklahoma. After marching much farther south, Long and his men moved eastward along a river they assumed to be the Red. They were, like Pike, mistaken; the watercourse they had followed at such great hardship, at one point becoming so reduced by starvation that they were forced to eat their own horses, proved to be the Canadian River.

Again like Pike's, Long's expedition has been denigrated as a fiasco, a meaningless exercise that contributed little significant or lasting knowledge. Long wrote that the plains "were almost wholly unfit for cultivation, and of course uninhabitable by a people depending on agriculture for their subsistence," thereby giving further credence to the notion of the Great American Desert. (Indeed, Long, rather than Pike, is sometimes given credit—or discredit— as the originator of this concept.) But Long was also one of the first Americans to insist on the importance of trained scientists as a part of any government exploring expedition, and among the curious cavalcade that accompanied him were Thomas Say, the nation's foremost zoologist and renowned even today as the father of American entomology, and Thomas Nuttall, who attempted the first comprehensive scientific classification of the West's botanical specimens. Titian Peale, son of the famous Philadelphia artist and scientist in whose Philadelphia museum Jefferson housed the gift grizzlies Pike had sent him until one of the bruins escaped, ran amok, and had to be destroyed, accompanied Long as the illustrator charged with artistically reproducing scientific specimens, which was an essential aspect of scientific exploring before photography was perfected. Samuel Seymour traveled with Long as the artist responsible for illustrating the official written report and is generally credited with being the first to paint and sketch the Rocky Mountains. In his use of scientists and artists—who were generally considered to be part of the scientific team—Long set a precedent for the conduct of future U.S. exploring expeditions.

But the most important breakthroughs in the American exploration of the Southwest were achieved by individuals acting in a private, rather than a public, capacity. In 1821, Mexico won its independence from Spain, whose rigid management of its colonial economy had been one reason for its colonists' discontent. The Mexican authorities soon let it be known that foreign traders would now be welcome in Santa Fe. That fall, three American trading parties from the east set out for New Mexico. One, led by Jacob Fowler and Hugh Glenn, followed the Arkansas River west from Fort Smith, in present-day Arkansas, to present-day Pueblo, Colorado, where they were then led southwest to Santa Fe by Spanish and Indian guides. A second, led by Thomas James and Robert McKnight, followed a similar route, while a third, led by William Becknell, rode west across the plains from Franklin, Missouri, to the Arkansas, then entered New Mexico via the Raton Pass, on the present-day border of New Mexico and Colorado.

All three expeditions found a ready market in Santa Fe for their goods—ribbon, spun cloth, whiskey, nails, rope, pepper, salt, tea, copper kettles, kitchen utensils, tobacco, knives, starch, and brooms—but the Becknell expedition was the most profitable and the most significant. Various difficulties—encounters with grizzly bears and belligerent

Indians, which cost the traders much of their stock and about half of their pack animals—lowered the profit margins of the other two expeditions, and the routes they traveled were indirect and impractical for large parties. Becknell, by contrast, made a profit of more than 400 percent, paid in gold, silver, and semiprecious stones, and on his return to Missouri he found a new route, via the Cimarron River, that would prove easily negotiable for even large wagon trains, as he demonstrated the next year when, accompanied by the soon-to-be legendary mountain men Joseph Walker, William Wolfskill, and Ewing Young, he returned to Santa Fe with many wagons filled with goods. His route would go down in history as the Santa Fe Trail; it would soon become so important to the economy of the West that just two years later Senator Thomas Hart Benton of Missouri sponsored a bill for the appropriation of funds to construct a federal road to the New Mexican trading center. (That same year Becknell led a train of 78 wagons, carrying $30,000 worth of goods, from St. Louis via his trail to Santa Fe, where they sold

Travelers whoop and wave their hats as their wagon train arrives at Santa Fe. The opening of the Santa Fe Trail marked the beginning of a new era in the history of the exploration and settlement of the Southwest.

for $180,000.) The completion of the Santa Fe road in 1827, along the basic route established by Becknell, represented the completion, in one sense, of the work begun by Pike. By 1831, 130 wagons traveled the trail annually.

As Americans began visiting the Southwest in number, they soon discovered that it was a much more diverse geographic area than the desert depicted by Pike and Long that is still the stereotypical image of the region held by many Americans. Much of the Southwest is desert, and in a much truer sense of the word than the Great Plains, but it also contains vast mountain ranges, verdant river valleys, and thick forests. At the same time that American merchants were flocking to Santa Fe, another kind of expectant capitalist was making his headquarters in that city and Taos, a smaller settlement to the northeast. These were the mountain men, as that brave, solitary breed of individuals who roamed the mountains and watercourses of the West in search of the valuable pelt of the beaver were known. In the course of their ramblings they added immeasurably to the store of geographic knowledge of the West.

Those mountain men who worked the southern range of the Rockies and carried their furs to Taos and Santa Fe for sale were known collectively as the Taos trappers. Among them was Wolfskill, a rugged Kentuckian who ranged as far west as the Rio Chama and the San Juan River in search of pelts; Young, a strapping Tennessean who may have reached the Wasatch and Uinta mountains just east of the Great Salt Lake and the desert and drainage region known as the Great Basin; and Etienne Provost, a rotund French Canadian who may have been the first white man to see the Great Salt Lake. One of the greatest of the so-called Taos trappers was James Ohio Pattie, although his achievements are sometimes discounted as little more than tall tales. In 1826, Pattie and two others, in company with a trapping party led by Ewing Young, traveled down the Gila River from present-day Phoenix, Arizona—Taos trappers usually reached the Gila by traveling

This picture is the only one taken from life of William Wolfskill, the mountain man and fur trapper who explored much of the Southwest. It was taken in 1866, the same year that Wolfskill died in Los Angeles.

west overland from the Rio Grande—to its junction with the Colorado, which they then followed north, becoming in the process the first white Americans to see the Grand Canyon. This natural marvel did not delay them long, however, for they continued up the Colorado to its source in the Rockies, crossed the mountains, picked up the Platte near its headwaters, and eventually reached the Bighorn and Yellowstone rivers.

At about the same time, other mountain men and Taos trappers were using the Gila to reach even farther west. In 1826, Jedediah Smith, perhaps the greatest of the mountain men, reached San Gabriel, California, after traveling south from the Great Salt Lake along the Virgin and Colorado rivers. A year later, Richard Campbell led a party of 35 trappers, via the Gila and the Colorado and much overland hiking, all the way to San Diego, a trek that Pattie duplicated just a few months later. In 1829,

The Grand Canyon is most likely the Southwest's greatest geographic marvel. This lithograph from 1892 represents the view from the canyon's south rim. Ewing Young and James Ohio Pattie, in 1826, were the first American explorers to see the canyon.

the redoubtable Young, aided by an adept teenage guide named Kit Carson, blazed a trail from Taos to San Gabriel, and Wolfskill and Thomas "Peg Leg" Smith led overland parties to California from New Mexico at about the same time. Armed with a small brass cannon strapped to a mule's packsaddle, Wolfskill's party became the first to reach California from New Mexico via an almost forgotten route known as the Old Spanish Trail, which took them by way of the Dolores, Sevier, Virgin, and Colorado rivers to the Pacific.

The ultimate rugged individualists, the mountain men carried on the work of western exploration at a time when the U.S. government, for various reasons, was less interested in doing so. Although it is undeniable that a love of the unknown was an integral part of their singular tem-

On September 13, 1847, U.S. forces stormed Chapultepec, a fortification that stood on a 200-foot-high rocky hill of the same name just southwest of Mexico City. The successful assault on Mexico City ensured a U.S. triumph in the Mexican War, and Mexico was forced to sell the United States the territory that is now known as the American Southwest.

perament, and that that curiosity, as old as humanity itself, to see what is beyond the hill on the horizon, or around the next bend of the river, must have informed their peripatetic wanderings, exploration in its purest sense—travel for the acquisition of knowledge—was rarely the mountain men's primary motive. Profit, not knowledge, probably figured foremost in that reckoning. Yet as the strange saga of Zebulon Pike demonstrates, and as an inquiry into the life and times of most of the great explorers would verify, exploration proceeds from motives as various and complex as the human character. Whether transmitted by word of mouth or sent in carefully prepared letters and maps to William Clark, who after his great western journey served as superintendent of Indian affairs in the West and acted as the semiofficial custodian of geographic data about the

A pass through the mountains of southern Arizona, by the artist John Mix Stanley, who accompanied U.S. forces commanded by Colonel Stephen Watts Kearny on their march from Santa Fe to the Pacific Coast after the outbreak of the Mexican War in 1846. Stanley's drawings were the first graphic representations of this part of the Southwest.

lands west of the Mississippi, the Taos trappers' travels and reports stimulated continued interest in the Southwest. By the 1840s, proponents of Manifest Destiny were clamoring for a war with Mexico for the region. The conflict that General James Wilkinson had so long anticipated, and that Zebulon Pike, knowingly or unknowingly, had worked to precipitate, finally broke out in May 1846. Two years later, by terms of the Treaty of Guadalupe Hidalgo, a victorious United States was sold the present-day states of New Mexico, Arizona, Colorado, Utah, Nevada, and California, and a new era of government-sponsored exploration of the Southwest, related to the business of settlement, began.

Further Reading

Abernathy, Thomas Perkins. *The Burr Conspiracy*. New York: Oxford University Press, 1954.

Adams, Samuel Hopkins. *The Santa Fe Trail*. New York: Random House, 1951.

Allen, John Logan. *Jedediah Smith and the Mountain Men of the American West*. New York: Chelsea House, 1991.

Batman, Richard. *American Ecclesiastes: The Stories of James Pattie*. San Diego: Harcourt Brace Jovanovich, 1984.

Carter, Carrol J. *Pike in Colorado*. Fort Collins, CO: Old Army Press, 1978.

Cavan, Seamus. *Lewis and Clark and the Route to the Pacific*. New York: Chelsea House, 1991.

Chittenden, Hiram Martin. *The American Fur Trade of the American West*. Vol. 2. New York: Harper, 1901.

Fehrenbach, T. R. *Lone Star: A History of Texas and the Texans*. New York: American Legacy Press, 1968.

Flores, Dan L. *Journal of an Indian Trader: Anthony Glass and the Texas Trading Frontier, 1790–1810*. College Station: Texas A&M University Press, 1985.

Goetzmann, William H. *Army Exploration in the American West 1803–1863*. New Haven: Yale University Press, 1959.

———. *Exploration and Empire: The Explorer and the Scientist in the Winning of the American West*. New York: Norton, 1966.

Gregg, Joseph. *Commerce of the Prairies*. Indianapolis: Bobbs-Merrill, 1970.

Hafen, LeRoy R., and Ann W. Hafen. *Old Spanish Trail*. Glendale, CA: Clark, 1954.

Hollon, W. Eugene. *The Lost Pathfinder: Zebulon Montgomery Pike.* Norman: University of Oklahoma Press, 1949.

Holmes, Kenneth L. *Ewing Young, Master Trapper.* Portland, OR: Binfords & Mort, 1967.

Jackson, Donald, ed. *The Journals of Zebulon Montgomery Pike with Letters and Related Documents.* Vols. 1 & 2. Norman: University of Oklahoma Press, 1966.

———. *Thomas Jefferson and the Stony Mountains: Exploring the West from Monticello.* Urbana: University of Illinois Press, 1981.

Jacobs, James Ripley. *Tarnished Warrior: Major-General James Wilkinson.* New York: Macmillan, 1938.

Nichols, Roger L., and Patrick L. Halley. *Stephen Long and American Frontier Exploration.* Newark: University of Delaware Press, 1980.

Smith, Page. *A People's History of the Ante-Bellum Years.* Vol. 4, *The Nation Comes of Age.* New York: McGraw-Hill, 1981.

Terrell, John Upton. *Zebulon Pike: The Life and Times of an Adventurer.* New York: Weybright and Talley, 1968.

Viola, Herman J. *Exploring the West.* Washington, DC: Smithsonian Books, 1987.

Chronology

The entries in roman type refer directly to Pike and the exploration of the American Southwest; entries in italics refer to important historical and cultural events of the era.

1773	*Backwoodsman Daniel Boone crosses the Appalachian Mountains and establishes a home in Kentucky, thus opening the door for westward expansion*
Nov.–Dec. 1775	*Aaron Burr makes the acquaintance of James Wilkinson while the two are serving with Benedict Arnold and the American expedition against Quebec*
July 4, 1776	*Declaration of Independence of the 13 colonies approved by the Continental Congress*
Jan. 5, 1779	Zebulon Montgomery Pike born in Somerset County, New Jersey
1794	Enlists in the army, joining the same company as his father; assigned quartermaster's duty
1799	Rises to the rank of full lieutenant under the wing of James Wilkinson
1800	*Spain cedes the Louisiana Territory to France*
1801	Pike marries Clarissa Brown, his cousin
1803	*The United States buys the Louisiana Territory from France for $15 million; the purchase extends American borders westward to the Rocky Mountains*
1804	*Meriwether Lewis and William Clark and their Corps of Discovery begin their two-year expedition from St. Louis up the Missouri River, across the Rocky Mountains, to the Pacific Coast*
Aug.–Dec. 1805	Pike dispatched by Wilkinson to travel to the upper reaches of the Mississippi to locate its source; under orders from Wilkinson, Pike also monitors British fur traders in the area; persuades the Sioux to sell 100,000 acres of land for $200 and future hunting rights

Feb.–April 1806	On reaching Lake Leech in northern Minnesota, Pike mistakenly proclaims it the source of the Mississippi; returns to St. Louis
July–Sept. 1806	Pike departs on his controversial western expedition
Oct.–Dec. 1806	Divides party at the Arkansas River; continues west toward mountains and Santa Fe; reaches Colorado; fails to climb Pikes Peak
Jan. 1807	Apparently lost, Pike halts the expedition on the upper Rio Grande
Feb. 1807	Pike and his men are taken to Santa Fe by Spanish troops to be questioned about their presence in New Spain
April–June 1807	The Americans are released by the Spanish and return to U.S. soil
1809	Wilkinson cleared of all charges of official malfeasance
April 27, 1813	Pike dies at the Battle of York
1821	Mexico wins its independence from Spain and allows foreign traders to operate in Santa Fe; William Becknell discovers trade route that will become the Santa Fe Trail
Dec. 1825	Wilkinson dies in Mexico City
1826	James Ohio Pattie and Ewing Young become the first white Americans to see the Grand Canyon; mountain man Jedediah Smith reaches San Gabriel, California
1846–48	*The United States defeats Mexico in war, thereby winning permanent control of the present-day states of Arizona, California, Colorado, Nevada, New Mexico, and Utah*

Index

American Revolution, 27, 29

Arkansas River, 13, 14, 17, 20, 21, 53, 55, 67, 69, 72, 81, 82, 85, 89

Arnold, Benedict, 22, 26

Becknell, William, 98, 99, 100

Benton, Thomas Hart, 99

Bonaparte, Napoléon, 35

Boone, Daniel, 35

Brown, James (father-in-law), 34

Brown, John, 72, 86

Burr, Aaron, 22, 26, 37, 41, 67, 91, 93, 94

Camino Real, 90

Campbell, Richard, 101

Chihuahua, Mexico, 90, 91

Chouteau, René Auguste, 38

Claiborne, William Charles Coles, 37

Clark, William, 39, 40, 54, 62, 93, 103

Cole, Nicholas, 90

Comanche, 54, 57, 62, 65, 71

Congress, U.S., 28, 37, 40, 53, 93

Conway Cabal, 26, 28

Daugherty, Thomas, 86, 87, 88, 91

Dearborn, Henry, 21, 40, 41, 48, 55, 67

Fernandez, Bartholomew, 88

Fort Washington, 28, 30, 31

Fowler, Jacob, 98

Gallatin, Albert, 94

Gates, Horatio, 26

George III, king of England, 41

Glenn, Hugh, 98

Grand Canyon, 101

Great American Desert, 60, 95, 97

Great Britain, 25, 26

Great Plains, 13, 60, 61, 65, 70, 100

Great Sand Dunes National Monument, 87

Gulf of Mexico, 35

Hamilton, Alexander, 22, 41

Humboldt, Alexander von, 89, 94

Itasca, Lake, 49

Jackson, Jeremiah, 87, 88

Jefferson, Thomas, 17, 21, 37, 38, 39, 40, 41, 53, 90, 94, 95

Kansas (tribe), 54, 61, 62, 63, 65

Kaskaskia, Illinois, 35, 42

La Lande, Baptiste, 56

Leech Lake, 49

Lewis, Meriwether, 39, 40, 42, 43, 53, 62, 95

Lisa, Manuel, 58–59

Long, Stephen Harriman, 60, 96, 97, 98

Louisiana Territory, 14, 19, 21, 35, 37, 39

McGillis, Hugh, 50, 51

McKnight, Robert, 98

Manifest Destiny, 44, 104

Meek, William, 88

Menaugh, Henry, 86, 87

Mexican War, 96

Mexico, 41, 98, 104

Miller, Theodore, 72, 88

Miro, Esteban, 29, 30

Mississippi River, 13, 21, 25, 28, 29, 31, 35, 37, 39, 41, 42, 45, 46, 47, 48, 49, 53, 54, 69, 95

Missouri River, 37, 40, 57

Montgomery, Richard, 26

Morrison, William, 56, 87

Mountain men, 100–103

New Mexico, 21, 54, 69, 87, 98

New Orleans, Louisiana, 28, 41

New Spain, 20, 21, 22, 25, 28, 29, 30, 37, 40, 41, 44, 53, 54, 55, 56, 57, 58, 62, 65, 67, 68, 69, 81, 87, 88, 90, 91, 94, 95, 96, 98

Nolan, Philip, 30

North West Company, 50–51

Nuttail, Thomas, 97

Ohio River, 28, 31, 34, 41

Old Spanish Trail, 102

Osage, 38, 40, 54, 56, 57, 58, 59, 61, 62, 63, 65

Osage River, 40, 57

Pattie, James Ohio, 100

Pawnee, 54, 61, 62, 63, 64, 65, 68, 69, 71

Peale, Titian, 97–98

Peter, George, 40, 41

Pike, Clarissa Brown (wife), 34, 35, 53, 95

Pike, George Washington
(brother), 27
Pike, Isabella Brown
(mother), 27
Pike, James Brown
(brother), 27
Pike, Maria Herriot (sister),
27
Pike, Zebulon (father), 27
Pike, Zebulon Montgomery
abilities as surveyor and
mapmaker, 53–54, 94
appearance, 31
Arkansas and Red rivers
expedition, 14–18, 19,
20–22, 53–91
death, 95
early military career,
30–35
early years, 26–28
education, 27, 32
Mississippi expedition,
41, 42, 43–51, 53–54,
55
relationship with James
Wilkinson, 28–29,
42–44, 93
Pikes Peak, 23, 72
Potawatomi, 30, 54
Provost, Etienne, 100

Red River, 14, 17, 21, 53,
55, 72, 81, 82, 86, 87,
88, 89, 90, 91, 97
Rio Grande, 88, 89
Robinson, John Hamilton,
55, 69, 72, 85–86, 87,
89, 90
Rocky Mountains, 35, 39,
53, 54, 70, 85, 89, 95,
97, 98, 100, 101
Royal Gorge, 81, 83

St. Louis, Missouri, 38, 39,
40, 41, 44, 45, 51, 53,
54, 56, 58, 68, 85, 99
Sangre de Cristo
Mountains, 21, 85
Santa Fe, 21, 55, 56, 57,
58, 59, 69, 72, 81, 87,
88, 89, 90, 96, 98, 99
Santa Fe Trail, 99–100
Say, Thomas, 97
Seymour, Samuel, 98
Sioux, 45, 47, 51, 97
Smith, Jedediah, 101
Smith, Patrick, 85, 88
Smith, Thomas "Peg Leg,"
102
Sparks, John, 86, 87, 88
Sugar Grove, Kentucky, 34

Taos, New Mexico, 100
Taos trappers, 100–102
Treaty of Guadalupe
Hidalgo, 104

Vasquez, Antoine F.
Baronet, 56, 85, 88

Walker, Joseph, 99
War of 1812, 30, 95
Washington, D.C., 35, 40
Wayne, "Mad" Anthony,
28, 30
White Wolf, 67, 68
Wilkinson, Ann Biddle, 14
Wilkinson, James, 14, 17,
19, 20, 21, 22, 26, 28,
29, 30, 34, 35, 37, 38,
40, 41, 42, 43–44, 46,
48, 53, 54, 55, 56, 57,
58, 67, 72, 88, 90, 93,
94, 95, 104
Wilkinson, James Biddle,
13, 15, 18–19, 20, 21,
57, 69
Wolfskill, William, 99,
100, 102

Young, Ewing, 99, 100,
102

Picture Credits

John James Audubon, Denver Public Library, Western History Department: p. 69 *Prairie Dogs*; Jules Bauman, courtesy of the Arizona Historical Society/Tucson: p. 101 *Looking Across the Main Canyon from the Rim of Hance Canyon* (#4282-C); The Bettmann Archive: p. 35; J. T. Bowen, courtesy of Missouri Historical Society, St. Louis: p. 36 *Le Soldat de Chene*; George Brewerton, the Oakland Museum Khan Collection: p. 80 *Jornada Del Muerto*; California State Library: p. 82 *San Juan Mountains in Winter*; George Catlin, Library of Congress: p. 19 *Buffalo Hunt* (USZ62-14157); Colorado Historical Society: pp. 16 *Arkansas River* (F#11597), 92 *Kit Carson* (F#1256); Denver Public Library, Western History Department: pp. 55, 81; Alexander Dick, Art Collection, Harry Ransom Humanities Research Center, University of Texas at Austin: p. 99 *Arrival of the Caravan at Santa Fe*; From a drawing by Seth Eastman, Art Collection, Harry Ransom Humanities Research Center, University of Texas at Austin: pp. 46–47 *Herd of Buffalo*; Seth Eastman, Library of Congress: p. 49 *Fort Snelling* (USZ62-4991); Theodore Gentilz, courtesy of the San Antonio Museum Association: p. 63 (detail from) *Comanches on the Warpath*; C. B. Graham, courtesy of the Museum of New Mexico: p. 23 (neg. #10118); H. W. Kemper, Library of Congress: p. 29 *Fort Washington* (USZ62-1878); Library of Congress: pp. 12 *Zebulon Pike* (USZ62-19731), 84 (USZ62-129), 102–3 *The Storming of Chapultepec* (USZ62-129); Robert Lindneux, courtesy of Colorado Historical Society: p. 24 *Zebulon Montgomery Pike* (F#4586); A. E. Mathews, Library of Congress: p. 71 *Pikes Peak and Colorado City* (USZ62-5494); Alfred Jacob Miller, Buffalo Bill Historical Center, Cody, WY: p. 50 *Louis–Rocky Mountain Trapper*; Alfred Jacob Miller, Walters Art Gallery, Baltimore: pp. 15 *Breakfast at Sunrise*, 48 *Expedition to Capture Wild Horses*, 64 *Pawnee Indians Migrating*, 67 *Roasting the Hump Rib*, 79 *Trapping Beaver*, 83 *Free Trappers in Trouble*; Courtesy of Missouri Historical Society: pp. 38 *Auguste Chouteau*, 52 *Osage Woman and Child*, 58 *Water Line and the Shores of the Ancient Lake* (from a drawing by Charles Koppel); Courtesy of the Museum of New Mexico: pp. 88 (detail from) *Santa Fe, New Mexico*, 89 (detail from) *Plaza La Mesilla*; Charles Willson Peale, Independence National Historic Park Collection: cover, pp. 40 *Meriwether Lewis*, 41 *William Clark*, 95 *Stephen Long*; Titian Ramsey Peale, American Philosophic Society: p. 77; Henri Penelon, courtesy of Frank Wolfskill: p. 100 *William Wolfskill*; Henry C. Pratt, University of Texas, Institute of Texan Cultures at San Antonio: p. 91 *The Plaza and the Church of El Paso*; Frederic Remington, Library of Congress: p. 87 (USZ62-50630); Frederic Remington, courtesy of Sid Richardson Collection of Western Art, Fort Worth, TX: p. 73 *Unknown Explorers*; Samuel Seymour, Amon Carter Museum, Fort Worth, TX: p. 96 *View of the Rocky Mountains on the Platte 50 Miles from Their Base*; Samuel Seymour, American, 1825, pen and watercolor, 4 3/8" x 8", gift of Maxim Karolik, courtesy of Boston Museum of Fine Arts: pp. 76–77 *View of James Peak in the Rain*; Samuel Seymour, Colorado Historical Society: p. 61 (F#34.236); Samuel Seymour, Kansas State Historical Society: p. 62; Samuel Seymour, Library of Congress: pp. 20 (detail from) *View of the Insulated Table Lands at the Foot of the Rocky Mountains* (USZ62-5341), 70 (detail from) *Distant View of the Rocky Mountains* (USZ62-5342); John Mix Stanley, Barker Texas History Center, University of Texas at Austin: p. 104 *First View of the Southwest*; John Mix Stanley, Phoenix Art Museum, museum purchase with funds provided by the estate of Carolann Smurthwaite: pp. 74–75 *Chain of Spires Along the Gila River*; Gilbert Stuart, Library of Congress: p. 34 *Thomas Jefferson* (USZ62-54129); Sir Anthony Van Dyke, Library of Congress: p. 26 *Aaron Burr* (USZ62-8322); Worthington Whittredge, *Santa Fe*, Yale University Art Gallery/gift from the estate of William W. Farnam to the Peabody Museum of Natural History: pp. 78–79; J. C. Wild, courtesy of Missouri Historical Society, St. Louis: p. 43 *View Of Front Street*

Jared Stallones is a high school teacher in Austin, Texas. He has a B.A. in liberal arts from the University of Texas, where he is currently working on a master's degree in education.

William H. Goetzmann holds the Jack S. Blanton, Sr., Chair in History at the University of Texas at Austin, where he has taught for many years. The author of numerous works on American history and exploration, he won the 1967 Pulitzer and Parkman prizes for his *Exploration and Empire: The Role of the Explorer and Scientist in the Winning of the American West, 1800–1900*. With his son William N. Goetzmann, he coauthored *The West of the Imagination*, which received the Carr P. Collins Award in 1986 from the Texas Institute of Letters. His documentary television series of the same name received a blue ribbon in the history category at the American Film and Video Festival held in New York City in 1987. A recent work, *New Lands, New Men: America and the Second Great Age of Discovery*, was published in 1986 to much critical acclaim.

Michael Collins served as command module pilot on the *Apollo 11* space mission, which landed his colleagues Neil Armstrong and Buzz Aldrin on the moon. A graduate of the United States Military Academy, Collins was named an astronaut in 1963. In 1966 he piloted the *Gemini 10* mission, during which he became the third American to walk in space. The author of several books on space exploration, Collins was director of the Smithsonian Institution's National Air and Space Museum from 1971 to 1978 and is a recipient of the Presidential Medal of Freedom.

J
B
PIKE,
ZEBULON

and the explorers
of the American
Southwest

LTON PUBLIC LIBRARY

00081 0890

Hamilton Public Library
South Hamilton, Massachusetts
01982